SAVE LIVES, ENJOY YOUR OWN

Finding Your Place in Medicine

BARBARA NICKEL HAMILTON, MD

ISBN: 978-1-7355468-0-3
Publishing Support Services by: Motivational M.D. Publishing

https://imreadytolaunch.com

Table of Contents

For F.E. and M.H., and those who
live their purpose.

And for Bob and Wesley, my personal
cheering squad at home.

Foreword

Sometimes the phone rings just after the first precious hour of sleep. The trauma surgeons need my help. When I rush into the hospital for an actively bleeding patient, I might not return home until dawn, but as I work, I'm in the zone. This work is a part of me. Being able to save a life is worth it every time. And I want *you* to find the kind of work that engages and fulfills you, too.

But how do you find the right field of medicine, in which you can harness your unique talents and skills? How do you find your calling while drinking from a fire hose? I'll address these important questions, with the help of some colleagues in various medical specialties.

Unfortunately, the male-dominated atmosphere, outdated ideas about what constitutes women's work, and concerns about work-life balance can discourage some women from surgically-oriented fields like my own. If your desired field is a boy's club, how do you figure out if you truly belong there? How do you navigate a sometimes foreign environment and succeed, despite the lack of female representation there?

If you dream of transforming from an uncertain student or trainee into one who confidently pursues her career path, you're in the right place. From the decision to work with your hands, to finding the right balance and learning to lead, this book will light the way. I'm so excited for you to join me as a physician who saves lives and enjoys her own!

Barbara Hamilton, MD

Introduction

Embarking on a medical career, I remember moments that made me second-guess my choice. I'll never forget being in medical school, relaxing at a bar with friends, and feeling like I'd educated myself out of the dating pool. The guys I talked to seemed to be confused or lose interest when I told them that I was a medical student. I learned not to mention it, or to say something euphemistic, like "I'm in healthcare," if they asked. They often assumed that "medical school" meant I was studying nursing, and I grew tired of correcting them. For the men in my class, though, being a medical student seemed to increase their allure to potential mates. Seeing this dynamic play out was one of the first experiences of gender bias in my career.

Later, in residency, after keeping quiet about my plans to pursue the male-dominated field of interventional radiology (IR), I confided in one of my attendings. "You're going to do IR?

Yeah right!" He exclaimed. These experiences surprised me and made me realize that society and medicine weren't nearly as progressive as I'd imagined. Luckily, that fact didn't deter me from pursuing my goals.

Inclusivity is at the heart of my mission because I believe it's still lacking in medicine. While I've been able to achieve some of my wildest dreams in my career, I'm not sure every qualified person will be so lucky. With this in mind, I was driven to start my blog in 2018. After transitioning to private practice and establishing myself as a physician within my local hospital system, I got married, had a baby, and bought a house. I felt like I'd arrived. And at that point, I felt compelled to share some of the lessons I'd gathered with the physicians who'd follow in my footsteps.

I felt compelled because when I was "growing up" in medicine, I had no idea what life would look like as a woman in a surgically-oriented field. In the later part of my training and in networking as an attending, I have been fortunate to meet many inspiring female colleagues. But in looking around online, I didn't see our perspective represented. I wanted to create a place where I could gather lessons together, where they could be found any time, by a trainee, perhaps someone like a younger version of myself. Someone who stood at a fork in the road, wondering which path to take.

I knew that by writing about my life as a "mom on call," I could help demystify the path, so it wouldn't be such a mystery what life was like for those aspiring to fields like mine. I named my blog TiredSuperheroine.com to showcase the different aspects of life as a physician who chooses to save lives and still enjoy her own. Because to me, "tired" can be a good thing: it can be the result of a day well-lived. As a new mom, there were times I was tired from waking up to breastfeed in the middle of the night. Other times, I've been taxed by a complex intervention, or from the extra few patients I saw that day. Sometimes, I've found myself emotionally tired from doctoring, only to be renewed by my two-year old's energy at home. I thrive between two worlds, because they balance each other. And I've found that each role has taught me to be better at the other.

So while your transition might look different from mine, this book can help guide you toward your place in medicine, where you can find the fulfillment you've worked so hard for. Whether you are about to enter medical school, are knee-deep in training, or are pivoting in your career, I hope this book provides the support you need to take the next step forward.

In the hospital halls and over late-night text messages, my female colleagues and I have shared the stories of our days. Over time, I began to realize we experienced similar challenges, despite practicing in different fields. And while many of us mentor trainees, I wondered, how many of these personal, off-the-cuff conversations are shared? That's the kind of wisdom I aim to share here. To that end, I've asked some of my colleagues in various procedural and surgical fields to contribute their thoughts and experiences. In these pages, you'll read about some of the important lessons they've learned along the way. While I hope to inspire you as part of the next generation of women in medicine, I'm not going to sugar-coat the challenges; they are real.

This book is written for women who aspire to procedural and male-dominated fields like my own. While the procedural subspecialties of medicine are different in many ways, the majority still share a common reputation: that of a boy's club. Whether the ranks of physicians practicing in those fields are mostly male, or men are over-represented in leadership, these kinds of environments can discourage female involvement, sometimes in insidious ways. Because women in these fields often face similar concerns and challenges, I believe we can learn from one another, and help each other out.

Although this book is written with aspiring and training female physicians in mind, I encourage you to share it with a male colleague when you're finished. There is value in sharing these ideas with our brothers in medicine, so they can join us as allies in the quest for gender equity. The act of passing this book along can help others to equip themselves with knowledge, so they can understand and support you in your medical journey. In this way, propagating knowledge and recruiting allies can have ripple effects for women in medicine at large.

Even though my focus is on female physicians, there are concepts here that will apply to other marginalized groups in medicine. Sadly, discrimination against such groups can mirror the marginalization they experience in society. And while I can't personally begin to address the systemic factors accounting for the low proportion of underrepresented minorities (URM) in medicine, we are working on it. Within the Society of Interventional Radiology (SIR), for example, numerous initiatives have been launched in an effort to improve upon the disparities in both physician representation and health outcomes in minority groups. These topics are of the utmost importance, with some health disparities in our country reaching crisis levels. These outcomes are interconnected with the lack of URM physicians in our medical system, which reinforces the distrust experienced by many of the patients within it. Since these disparities are connected, they must each be addressed to affect real change. I speak to some of these topics on my blog at https://tiredsuperheroine.com.

I also write this book with the awareness that for some people in medicine, male, female, and non-binary, the road is just harder. Whether for having to surmount the circumstances of their upbringing or for having a nonconforming gender or sexual identity-- for the underrepresented, unseen, and unacknowledged who strive to make a difference for your future patients, I am writing this for you, too.

And a final note before we get started. There are journaling prompts at the end of each chapter, to help prime you for the greatness you're about to achieve. I call these Spill Your Guts journaling exercises. In doing so, I do not make light of the work we do as women who operate. Instead, I hope you'll see this as a nod to the sometimes sardonic humor that gets many health workers through the day. If you're not yet acquainted with this peculiar kind of humor, you soon will be. In medicine, as we face life and death, this brand of humor can serve as a pressure relief valve. Welcome aboard.

"Don't ever let somebody tell you you can't do something...

[If] You got a dream, you gotta protect it. When people can't do something themselves, they're gonna tell you that you can't do it.

You want something, go get it. Period."

(The Pursuit of Happyness, 2006)

CHAPTER 1

Finding Your Place: Why It Matters

A well-groomed man, towering six and a half feet tall, arrived at my office for a consultation. We were meeting to discuss the removal of his vena cava filter, which I implanted several months prior when he suffered an episode of pulmonary embolism. At that time, I helped to break up the clots in his lungs by placing small tubes in each of his lung arteries under live x-ray, to deliver a potent enzyme therapy. Just as I'd been taught in training, I shaped the stiff back-end of my wire between my thumb and second finger, allowing me to direct my catheter through his heart and into his lungs, where I'd carefully exchange for specially-designed infusion catheters. Delivering these devices allowed me to dissolve the clot quickly and safely, decreasing the burden on his heart and lungs. His chest pain and shortness of breath subsided overnight as the treatment took effect. As the patient strode toward my office that day, I almost didn't recognize him as he took my hand and said, "Hi Doctor. Thanks for saving my life."

As a physician, you'll soon experience moments like these. Practicing medicine is an unbelievable privilege, and I'm thrilled to welcome you on your journey. Over the course of medical school and training, you'll join the ranks of professionals like you, who dedicate their lives to the health of others. In doing so, you will stand with some of the smartest and most hard-working people you will ever meet.

But despite the commonalities among medical students, you'll notice that during the first two years of your medical education, there will be some people you jive with, and others you don't. In my class of one hundred forty students, people gravitated together to form little cliques, some of which still exist to this day. It's not uncommon to hear of a close friendship or even marriage that started in the anatomy lab. Some of my own bonds from medical school have lasted over ten years now, and some may last a lifetime. So it's possible this social grouping isn't such a bad thing. Given the limited time you have to socialize, and the intense, formative period you'll share together, these med school friendships can become treasures. During these years, I encourage you to broaden your circle by meeting as many people as you can. And even as you face the pressures of medical school, approach these budding friendships with gratitude.

During the clinical years, as you rotate through each specialty and choose a career path, the process of organizing into groups becomes formalized. Each clinical rotation and elective can come to feel like a courting period. As you temporarily assume the role of a student-doctor in that specialty, you'll try to figure out: are these my people? Could I commit to this kind of work for life?

Get ready to discover fields you never knew existed. There may be specialties you're not aware of yet that catch your attention during the clinical years. That's what happened to my colleague, Dr. Annie Gill, a pediatric interventional radiologist at Emory University. "I was considering surgery: specifically breast, vascular, and pediatric surgery when one of my mentors suggested I look into interventional radiology (IR). After learning more about IR, I became more and more interested. I decided to do a rotation early in my fourth year of medical school, and fell in love with the field."

Finding Where You Belong While Drinking from a Fire Hose

One of my Deans used to liken medical education to drinking from a fire hose. Over the course of four years, you'll learn an entirely new language, made up of Greek and Latin roots, not to mention countless microbial organisms, pathologies, and drugs. This language will help you communicate on the wards in the clinical years, enabling you to become acquainted with the new and varied disciplines of medicine. These rotations will allow you to see the mass of knowledge below the "tip of the iceberg." And after a brief introduction to each specialty, you'll be expected to commit to one.

Choosing your career path in medicine is a major decision, and it's one you'll make under duress. While learning as much and as fast as you can, you'll find where you belong. Because of the time course and the stressors involved, it's sort of a miracle when it goes right. That's why I hope this book can serve as a resource as you make this important personal decision.

Looking back at my experience on the wards, some rotations flowed, while others were a grind. When things were going well, I felt engaged and accepted; I could rise to any challenge. For me, this seemed to happen in the surgical fields, from obstetrics (OB) to urology and general surgery. When I struggled, it was often when I felt less engaged, whether due to the subject matter, the environment, or a combination thereof. In internal medicine and pediatrics, for example, I didn't seem to speak the same language as the other physicians, and it seemed to make everything harder. Beyond individual personality differences, when I simply didn't fit into the culture of a given specialty, it became pretty clear. The end result was a situational sense of malaise, and predictably, a lackluster grade on that rotation.

A medical career can be consuming, requiring your time, focus, and emotional energy-- so it's worth finding your sweet spot within it. When you do, you'll find like-minded people who understand you, and who can help you fulfill your potential. Dr. Nancy Yen Shipley, an orthopaedic surgeon, shares how she felt as she discovered her place in medicine. "I was considering plastic surgery, but then realized it wasn't entirely for me. It's a little intangible when you start rotating with different groups [of physicians]. I really liked the plastic surgeons... but it wasn't until I got into my ortho rotations that I felt like, 'Oh my gosh, *these* are my people, and this is clearly where I belong.'"

In this book, you'll hear about my own experiences, alongside those of my colleagues in various procedural and surgical fields. I hope these accounts supplement your experience on the wards, where you may not always have a female role model or mentor to guide you.

In medical school and training, you'd be wise to follow your inner compass as you attempt to absorb everything happening around you. In these formative years, any moment can unexpectedly provide insight into your future career if you're open to it. It was during a second-year pathophysiology lecture that I encountered my future field for the first time. On the other hand, if you're like most students, you may not find or settle on your specialty until the third or fourth year of medical school, when you've had a chance to experience your options first-hand. Whether you enter medical school with an idea of a future specialty or not, I recommend seeking electives in specialties you otherwise wouldn't gain exposure to. For example, if you know that you have an affinity for procedures, look to the procedurally-oriented subspecialties of medicine and surgery, like critical care, gastroenterology, urology, or radiology (among many others). The more fields you try on, the better your chance of finding the right fit for you.

Finding your Place as an Attending Physician

When you complete your years of training, you'll finally be poised to practice independently, using your hard-earned skills to help your patients. But there will still be challenges. There will be times when a difficult patient, staff member, or complication will push you to the limits of what you feel you can handle. That's when dedication to your work can help keep you going. At my own institution, I've had countless challenges from poor hospital infrastructure to the excessive turnover of support personnel. In a way, these hardships have strengthened my conviction to do what I can to improve the system and to provide a high level of care to the patients who need me.

There will be days in which you feel like you're choosing patient care over your own family; that's when it's critical that the work fulfills you. When my day runs long, I eat alone in the hospital cafeteria, refueling for my last few cases. Meanwhile, my husband and son might be eating too, just a few miles away. But because I love what I do, I take time off to rest, and I otherwise have ample time with my family, it's okay. Even those extended days are a part of the plan.

Other times, the phone rings after midnight. As I turn on my computer and wait groggily for a patient's images to load, I can feel the weight of my role. I've trained for this moment when my fellow physicians need my help. If I need to address an emergency, like an actively bleeding patient, I might not return home until dawn. But as I work, I'm in the zone. This work is a part of me. Being able to stop someone's bleeding is worth it every time. And you'll share this kind of mission-driven satisfaction with others in your field, who know exactly how it feels.

Your People Will Support You

Perhaps you have known for some time that you're a doctor in the making. Whether you have wanted to become a doctor since you were a kid, or were inspired to pursue medicine after the illness of a family member, there is a deep drive that propels many of us through our medical careers.

But despite that inner drive, and the endless stream of patients who need help, you must remember you are not a machine. Despite medical training, which pushes us to our limits, we must remember to rest and take care of ourselves. We must remember that sometimes, we will fail. Despite the expectations of patients and families, there are limits to what we can do as physicians; we can't "fix" or save every patient. When you're driven by a deep connection to your work, these challenges are worth facing. And no one will understand that better than the people working alongside you. "It's important to find supportive colleagues, because being a physician is challenging and demanding," according to Dr. Arghavan Salles, an academic surgeon. "Without social support, it is difficult to manage stressors and provide the best care."

As you experience the highs and lows of a medical career-- some of which I'll describe in chapters to come-- you'll call on others for help. Sometimes you'll ask a colleague or mentor for advice, while other times, you'll be the one to provide support. Together, you will weather the challenges and triumphs in medicine. As a result of the camaraderie you share, your medical colleagues will sometimes understand in a way your friends or family can't. In this way, your colleagues become like a family, too. This is the value of finding your people in medicine.

Your quest in medicine will require you to look inward. To assist you in the process, I've included some questions at the end of each chapter. You can write your responses in a journal, on a sheet of scrap paper, or in the margins of this book. I've dubbed these "Spill Your Guts" exercises, with the hope that you'll hold nothing back. Write whatever comes to mind, without judgment or censoring yourself. Take your time, and write until it's all on the page. If you write until your hand aches, you might be onto something.

These exercises will dig for the insights you hold within. They may be buried under your mental to-do list right now, but they are waiting to be noticed and explored. Together, we can start to examine any beliefs that could be holding you back. Through these pages, I will encourage and challenge you to find your rightful place in medicine.

Spill Your Guts

- Have you been a part of or seen any particular social groups in your educational journey so far?
  - Have these been beneficial or detrimental?
  - Give a couple of examples.
- Name a recent time in which you leaned on a friend for support.
  - How did it feel?
- In your experience in the medical field so far, have you felt like you belong?
  - Why or why not?

CHAPTER 2

Finding Your People in Medicine

So how do you go about finding the right fit in medicine? Part of finding your place is finding the people you connect with. As an example, I'm an interventional radiologist (IR). My field is comprised of physicians who use minimally-invasive techniques to navigate through the body under image guidance. Unlike traditional surgery, we use stealthy devices, narrower than the diameter of a pencil to do our work, rather than incisions. We can use these tools inside the blood vessels to reopen an artery that's become occluded by cholesterol and calcified plaque. The techniques we use often allow for a quicker recovery and decreased peri-procedural risk. In our technologically and device-driven field, we even share a specialty-specific slang, which describes the unique feel to our work, and the tools we use to perform it. Because of these commonalities, we tend to share many of the same values around patient care, speak the same language, and find ourselves on the same wavelength. This is what it's like to find your kin in medicine.

But initially, it wasn't clear that these were my people. When I encountered IR for the first time, even as a taller-than-average woman, I felt small, almost negligible. I was surrounded by towering men, a stereotypical scenario in my specialty. Beyond that surface observation, however, I felt highly engaged by what was happening in the procedure suite. Despite initial appearances, it became clear: I did belong there.

Some time later, our group comprised of attendings, trainees, and students mulled over a clinical question. I looked up the answer and emailed it to my attending, who happened to be the fellowship director. He was so impressed by my initiative, that he asked my mentor about my residency application. While this action required no stroke of genius on my part, it demonstrated interest. And when I heard that I'd impressed my attending, I felt like I'd won the lottery. The excitement I felt-- the feeling of being "turned on" by a field-- is a clue that you might enjoy a career in it. So despite my initial misgivings about fitting in, I felt welcomed and invited to pursue my interest further.

Finding Your People as an Individual

Becoming a certain kind of specialist doesn't mean becoming a clone within the group. You don't have to look or act like other members of your specialty in order to belong. Despite the pervasive stereotypes that remain in medicine, members of a specialty are still individuals. While you might share some similarities with others in your field, you aren't required to hang out with them on the weekend or share all of the same interests. And being different from other members of the group shouldn't preclude finding the support and mentorship you need. As Dr. Annie Gill notes, "Despite not having a single female role model in IR, I continued to love the field. This was not a deterrent for me. Even though some of my role models were very different from me, they were still incredibly beneficial and supportive."

As you find your people, you'll take on a new identity: that of a physician. In this new role, you will use medical knowledge, skills, and a spirit of service to help your patients. You'll take on new responsibilities, and interact with countless patients and hospital staff. In this role, you'll get to know yourself within the culture of medicine, and find what drives you. As Dr. Nikki Keefe, a recently graduated interventional radiology fellow at the University of Virginia shared: "Everyone takes on a new identity as they begin to feel like a doctor. Whether I'm headed to the clinic or the angio room, I'm driven by my responsibility to the next patient. That's why, when I start walking faster and more purposefully than I normally would, my husband jokingly calls it my "doctor walk."

An Identity in Transit

As you become this new version of yourself, it's natural to feel vulnerable. Becoming a doctor is demanding, requiring incredible amounts of time, energy, and brainpower. The transition can push you beyond what you've experienced before. And if you're like me, you might be overwhelmed by it at times. In med school and training, as I climbed the steepest parts of the learning curve, I sometimes felt like I was just hanging on, as I struggled to keep up with the pace of what was happening around me. For this reason, I shared very little about my personal life. Coming from a non-medical family, I was worried that I lagged behind and that students from medical families intrinsically knew more than I did. They often seemed to live more comfortably, too, as I scrimped and saved, fretting over my growing student loan balances. I didn't want others to notice that I was different, for fear I'd be seen as inferior or unworthy, so I kept a low profile. In reality, the majority of my classmates struggled with the challenging coursework to varying degrees, too, and most of them had loans like me. The perception I had was partly due to fear.

Women and under-represented minorities (URM) in procedural and surgical fields can likewise have a hard time fitting in, and at worst, face discrimination. That's why it's important to have social support outside of the hospital, too. Dr. Susan O'Horo, an interventional radiologist in Massachusetts confided that there were many periods in her career in which she stifled her personality at work. "All the time," she said. "I would say I am more fun outside of work. I think it is important to maintain a professional persona within the hospital. That's why I prefer to relax and have a good time outside of work."

Dr. Aneesa Majid adds, "I have a chosen family in medicine, mostly women from my training days and those I have become close with over the years. I also have a close group of non- medical friends; that is equally important. You would be surprised how many of the issues we face as women in medicine are mirrored in other industries. Sometimes, having different perspectives applied to a situation can be helpful in navigating it. I call on my friends all the time, to vent, to listen to them, to walk through challenges-- particularly big decisions, like leaving a practice, starting a new practice, negotiating a contract-- just about everything."

As a physician, you will have to decide how much of yourself you bring into your professional persona. As a trainee, as I began to get to know and trust those around me, I became willing to share more of myself with others. In turn, my mentors became more invested in me and my future. And it wasn't as frightening as

I'd imagined it would be. Drs. O'Horo and Majid agree that it's important to have supportive people outside of medicine too-- especially if you find you're not bringing all of yourself to work just yet.

Becoming yourself in medicine is a process that can evolve over the course of your career; there's no need to rush it. Like peeling the layers of an onion, you can accomplish this gradually, one step at a time. Six years into my attending role, I share more of myself at work than I used to. That's because I've become more comfortable in my role over time. So when things are running smoothly, I partake in small-talk with the staff, getting to know them incrementally. Being a three-dimensional physician can foster a more open atmosphere, in which everyone on the team learns to understand each other better. So if you're feeling constricted in your role as a trainee, know that it can and often does become easier with time, especially as you settle into an attending role.

As a trainee, you might wonder how much of yourself you can actually bring to work. This depends on your personality as well as your environment. It helps to gauge how much others around you are sharing. Opening up to others always entails a small risk. But when appropriate, the connection it brings can be well worth it. Deciding how much of yourself to share is a judgment call. For now, know that it's OK to hold back a bit if that feels easier. Take comfort in knowing that it's part of the process of maturing into and gaining confidence in your role.

Feeling like the Odd Woman Out

As a female physician in a procedural or surgical field, you might find that sometimes, you're the only woman around. When I asked Dr. Nancy Yen Shipley about finding her place in a male-dominated field, she said, "Finding like-minded people was definitely a part of my choosing orthopaedic surgery. Although I didn't have many female mentors at that point, I got along pretty well with the other students going into ortho, and the ortho residents, which were mostly guys. So it's not that I was uncomfortable in that setting. But every once in a while, I'd look around and say to myself, 'Huh, I'm the only female here.'"

I've had the same realization in my career, and depending on the field you choose, you may as well. In fellowship training, I was the only female out of six fellows. There were rumors that just one female fellow was allowed in the program each year. And while my co-fellows and I all bonded in a way, I sometimes felt like an outsider looking in, as the others developed close, brotherly bonds. Though I suspected I was as smart as my co-fellows, I still doubted myself a lot.

At the end of the year, I gave my favorite attending a gift. He had a great sense of humor and served as a kind and steady anchor for me during that tough fellowship year. Since his focus was on venous procedures, we had often done venous sampling cases together, collecting samples of blood from different locations of the body, to help locate occult hormone-producing tumors. That's why, when I found a figurine of a cartoonish vampire creature clutching a blood-filled syringe, it seemed the perfect gift. Despite the hesitation I felt, I took a risk and gave him the figurine, hoping he'd see it as a humorous gesture of appreciation. He accepted it with a smile that said, "Thanks, crazy lady..." But years later, the memory of that quirky gift reminds me that, in my own way, maybe I belonged all along.

Spill Your Guts

- 🐚 Think back to some moments in school or training in which you clicked with people right away.
  - ▫ Where were you?
  - ▫ Who were you with?
  - ▫ What were you doing?
- 🐚 Were there any rotations or situations that just didn't feel right, or where you struggled to fit in?
  - ▫ Why or why not?
- 🐚 Which situations or rotations made you feel energized or excited?

CHAPTER 3

Wanna Operate?

One of the joys of the procedural fields is learning to use your dexterity to help patients. In the context of this book, I use the term "operate" in a general sense, to include more than the traditional methods of surgery. In using this term, I'm speaking of the ability to use manual skills to perform medical procedures, whether there's an incision involved or not. The way I use it includes procedures like endoscopy and intubation, arteriography, and laparoscopy, just to name a few examples.

If you're not yet familiar with these terms, endoscopy involves inserting a camera through the mouth or anus to visualize the bowel from the inside, where a gastroenterologist or surgeon can perform procedures like polypectomy or biopsy, among others. Intubation involves inserting a tube through a patient's mouth into the trachea, or windpipe. Physicians with this skill include emergency physicians, intensivists, and anesthesiologists. Arteriography involves taking direct images of blood vessels using dense liquid contrast under x-ray. This can be performed by IR, vascular surgery, or cardiology. Finally, laparoscopy is a less invasive method of traditional surgery, which involves inserting instruments through small holes in the abdomen, avoiding the need for larger incisions.

Each of these examples involves a great deal of skill and judgment on the part of the operator. Procedures like these take place in various operating room (OR) or OR-like environments. As women who operate, we can experience similar challenges in our careers, some of which relate to working in male-dominated spaces. It's for this reason that I believe we stand to learn a lot from one another.

Whether you've chosen your specialty or not, you may have an idea of whether you enjoy procedures. Personally, I find them to be gratifying and integral to my work. If you're not sure yet whether you have "good hands," or would like to focus on procedures in your career, figuring this out is a good place to start your search. Deciding to focus on or de-emphasize procedures in your work can help to narrow down your options as you find your place in medicine.

I hadn't always planned on a surgically-oriented career; instead, I stumbled into one. Growing up in a relatively healthy, non-medical family, I had limited exposure to different medical fields. My view of medicine was therefore shaped by annual visits to the family doctor, an occasional trip to the dermatologist, and coming of age in the '90s, the hit TV drama, "ER." By the time I encountered radiology in a second-year pathophysiology lecture, I was surprised by how different it was from the doctoring I'd seen, and I was spell-bound by the skills involved. The lecturer, a female Program Director, and a mother of four would become my future mentor.

During her lecture, she grabbed my full attention. By the time I encountered my first image-guided procedure on a radiology elective, I was hooked. I watched as an IR cursed his way through a fistulagram, and thought, *This guy is a wizard.* Using access points measuring just a couple of millimeters in diameter, he was able to troubleshoot and re-open a clotted dialysis access in the arm, which was previously fashioned by a vascular surgeon. As he navigated through the patient's body to fix the problems he found, I realized I wanted to become an interventional radiologist one day.

Many of us who've found our calling relate to the wonder experienced by Dr. Nancy Yen Shipley when she shadowed an orthopaedic surgeon for the first time. "It was between my first and second years of medical school that I spent a week with a total joint surgeon. I was surprised to see how invasive, almost violent, a total hip replacement was. Fortunately, I shadowed long enough to see the patient return for their first post-operative visit, upright and walking. It was striking, and I really came to appreciate the return to function after seeing that."

As women who operate, we are able to treat the problems we diagnose in a tangible way. And the kind of gratification that results extends across different procedural specialties. Whether you find this kind of work satisfying is one component of figuring out if you want to operate for a living.

Dexterity: The Foundation of a Procedural Specialist

The first Nintendo gaming system came out the year I was born, and I spent much of my childhood playing video games. As I leaped through The Super Mario Brothers series, I developed my dexterity and an affinity for using my hands in this way. Years later, when I was handed a cystoscope for the first time on a urology rotation, it felt familiar. As I manipulated the instrument, I realized decades-old muscle memory was helping me learn a new medical procedure. The urologist noticed my potential and encouraged me to join his ranks. Even now, when people struggle to understand what I do as an interventional radiologist, I use the video game analogy. It captures the heart of image-guided procedures, and why they are so fun.

Don't get me wrong-- I had no talent for sports requiring hand-eye coordination. So if you're thinking, "I'm not coordinated enough to do procedures," don't be discouraged. Instead of playing sports like softball or basketball, I worked on my fine motor skills as I knitted "cobra" bracelets from plastic lanyard, a popular activity when I was a kid. If you enjoyed sewing or crafting growing up, those talents could translate to procedural dexterity as well.

Dr. Arghavan Salles had similar interests as a kid. "I've always enjoyed working with my hands! Growing up, I played piano, crocheted, knitted, and played video games," she told me. Dr. Lola Oladini, an IR in training, also played piano in her formative years. She came to value the meditative nature of playing: "Somehow it was relaxing to take a deep breath, stop consciously thinking, and let my fingers flow across the keys." And that wasn't the only dexterous skill she honed. "As a Nigerian, my mom emphasized the importance of knowing how to braid hair, telling me I'd need to braid my own daughter's hair one day. So I started braiding and styling hair, too. Both of these activities required fine motor skill, yet felt relaxing and easy to me. They likely provided the foundation for my wanting to work with my hands in my career."

But... Blood? Body fluids? No thanks...

Maybe you like the idea of operating but worry you might be squeamish. Growing faint or disgusted by certain unpleasant stimuli is an involuntary reaction thought to be tied to empathy. So don't be ashamed if you get light-headed in a surgical setting. Luckily, this phenomenon, also known as a vasovagal reaction, is one you can manage and even extinguish over time. Repeated exposure can habituate you to certain triggers so that you gradually become less sensitive to them. Certain factors can make you more prone to a reaction, like low blood sugar, dehydration, and fatigue. So if you're still getting used to the operating room environment, it's important to take preventative measures, like drinking adequate fluids, eating, and getting rest when you can, especially before long operations.

I know what it's like to be squeamish because I've grappled with this kind of reaction myself. During a phlebotomy lecture in medical school, my hearing went fuzzy, and my peripheral vision darkened, as I hovered at the edge of consciousness. I slumped in my seat until my vision returned a few minutes later. I felt silly that this was happening to me in medical school, and worried about what it might mean for my future as a physician.

Later, near the end of my OB rotation, I almost hit the floor during a cesarean section, as warm amniotic fluid exploded onto our booties. Despite having seen multiple surgeries at that point, my blood sugar was low, and it made me vulnerable to a vasovagal episode. Thankfully, I've extinguished this reaction over time, and though I still don't want to perform a c-section myself, I'll gladly help out with a post-partum embolization (a procedure to stop uncontrolled bleeding through the uterine arteries) when it's needed.

Now, as an interventional radiologist, my work centers around the use of long needles, which I use to puncture blood vessels and solid organs all over the body. After a case, my hands and gown can be stained with a patient's blood. But when I'm focused on my work, my squeamishness is a thing of the past. So if you find yourself faint early on, it doesn't have to stop you from pursuing a procedural path. Take the precautions mentioned above, and most of all, don't be ashamed. This is a very common phenomenon.

Reactions of this kind can even be a good thing if you believe my first clinical preceptor, Dr. Bora. A plastic surgeon, he shepherded me through the first surgical experiences of my third year. Our first procedure together was a rhinoplasty, or "nose job." I scrubbed in and acclimated to the new operating room (OR) environment. But as he hammered the girl's nasal septum, I began to have that familiar wobbly feeling. Mercifully, the OR nurses rescued me, offering a seat nearby, so I didn't have to break scrub. After a few moments, I was able to collect myself and return to the operating table.

After the case, I waited for admonishment for my obvious display of weakness. But my preceptor belly-laughed, declaring my reaction was a good sign. "That means it turns you on!" He bellowed. In spite of my faintness, he encouraged me to consider a career in surgery. So in case you're in a less supportive environment than I was, let me reassure you-- just because you get squeamish, it doesn't mean you have to rule out the surgically-oriented fields.

What Kind of Work Lights You Up?

There is a wide array of options to choose from in the world of medicine, each with its own environment and patient population. Perhaps you're interested in pulmonary/ critical care or anesthesia and enjoy the immediacy of placing an arterial line or endotracheal tube. Or, perhaps you have an affinity for robotically-assisted genitourinary surgeries, and the outcomes they provide for patients with incontinence.

For me, navigating through the body using minimally-invasive, image-guided techniques will never get old. In my field, my experience paired with visual and tactile feedback tell me when I've punctured the portal vein in a TIPS (transjugular intrahepatic portosystemic shunt) procedure. Because of the scarring of the liver in cirrhosis, venous blood returning to the liver backs up in the gut, causing elevated venous pressures, and often, as a result, life-threatening bleeding. The purpose of a TIPS is to redirect some of the blood flow from the liver back to the heart. As I perform this challenging procedure, I get a thrill as my wire slithers into the portal vein, securing my new access. And, I'm deeply satisfied by a well-positioned stent-graft. Under fluoroscopic, or live x-ray guidance, other kinds of specialists, from vascular surgeons, cardiologists, and others, likewise learn to interpret the images which guide us through the human body.

For me, even the simplest "bread and butter" procedures are rewarding. The most common procedures become old friends over time. Yet even a simple procedure can humble you in an instant. In a central line placement, when your wire unexpectedly shows up on the wrong side of the screen, you might wonder if you've cannulated the carotid artery instead of the jugular vein. Or, you could be dealing with an anatomic variant, like a left-sided superior vena cava. In an arteriogram, a vessel selection can become challenging due to the patient's anatomy. Situations like these prompt you to think quickly and problem-solve on the fly. As you break a sweat and reach for a different catheter, you might solicit ideas from the room. This experience is integral to your growth as a woman who operates.

Spill Your Guts

- Do you envision yourself working with your hands in your career?
  - Why or why not?
- When you think of the most fascinating careers you've encountered, is there anything holding you back from pursuing them, based on what you've heard, seen, or experienced?
- What are some of the procedures you would love to learn?
- Are there specific patients or disease processes you'd like to work within your career?

CHAPTER 4

Wanna Save Lives?

As we've discussed, many proceduralists and surgeons learn to diagnose problems and fix them. Sometimes, the problem at hand can be life-threatening. Being on staff at a trauma center, I attend to emergencies regularly. A common call might involve a motorcycle accident with a pelvic crush injury, for example. IRs like myself are often involved when injuries like these arise since the affected arteries can be small, difficult to visualize, or inaccessible at surgery. That's when angiography, direct imaging of the blood vessels, is indicated. Using thin plastic tubes guided by wires, my team and I navigate through the vessels to find the site of bleeding and treat it, injecting surgical gel foam in the affected artery or sometimes, leaving a small metallic coil to block blood flow permanently. We can often see the effects of our work right away, with the patient's vital signs stabilizing on the table.

It takes a team of physicians to care for patients like these. Specialists of different stripes use their complementary skills; from the EMTs (emergency medical technicians) and emergency physicians who receive these patients to the trauma surgeons, vascular surgeons, and orthopaedists-- we all work together to save life and limb. When one specialist reaches his or her limit, they can ask another for help. In the case of trauma care, a partnership between specialists is key to obtaining the best possible outcome for the patient.

Making a Difference Through Your Work

No matter the skills you'll use, being able to treat the problems you find is the kind of instant gratification non-procedural docs can only dream of. And what could be better than saving a life? It's no exaggeration to say that I get to save lives routinely in my work.

I'll never forget the time I checked on my patient with a bleeding ulcer after our procedure. I had blocked off (embolized) the vessel supplying the ulcer, saving his life in the process. He was an anxious fellow to begin with, and he was recovering from the near-death experience. As I entered the room, he grasped my hand, kissing it repeatedly, proclaiming his love for me in a thick Russian accent, as his lovely wife stood by, shaking her head in relief. Saving a patient's life has a ripple effect on everyone they know-- in this case, on the man's young children, who would continue to grow up with a father. The effect you can have on others' lives is part of the magic of these fields and why we work so hard to master them. But they aren't for everyone, and only you can decide for yourself. Are you willing to come to the bedside at all hours of the day and night? Plenty of emergencies, especially traumas, happen after midnight when the bars close and people's judgment falters.

Lola Oladini, MD, MBA, a resident in interventional radiology reflects on the dichotomy of being on call: "It's a privilege to be in the hospital late at night. When I'm walking through empty hallways toward the call room, I feel like a Watchman (woman) of sorts. It feels like I'm serving so others can have peace and good health. I think service is my calling, so I usually don't mind. Of course, I still get tired, and occasionally frustrated with calls as a resident."

As you consider whether you want to include emergencies in your career, you should be aware of some myths surrounding certain specialties, especially the traditionally male-dominated and procedural fields. A common one is that women shouldn't go into these fields because of the lifestyle. Ironically, some suggest women should avoid fields that involve waking up in the middle of the night when traditional female roles such as motherhood require waking frequently throughout the night. If your ideal life doesn't include waking up in the middle of the night, you may want to avoid emergency call-- and newborns, for that matter. Ultimately, these decisions are up to you as an individual. In this day and age, they shouldn't hinge on your gender.

It's up to you what kind of call, and the frequency of call you'd prefer, to a degree. For example, some students choose to pursue fields in which emergencies are less common, like ophthalmology. Others may desire a clear demarcation between their work and home lives, opting for specialties with shift-work, like emergency medicine or critical care. In fields like these, you can attend to emergencies on your shift, then go home after handing off to the next doctor. As an IR at my institution, being responsible for the service for a week at a time is manageable, and allows for improved continuity of care. In the end, the decision to attend emergencies is a personal one.

In evaluating your willingness to fill such a role, you must decide:

- Are you someone who enjoys rescuing?
- Do you remain focused in a crisis?
- Do you perform well under pressure?
- Will you be able to care for yourself in the face of a sometimes erratic schedule, or the occasional loss of sleep?

If you thrive on a bit of stress as I do, you might be great in an emergency. You could be a life-saver.

Facing Death

In the course of your career choice, you might wonder: Am I ready to face death, personally and/or professionally? Attending to life-threatening emergencies requires a degree of emotional detachment-- enough that would allow you to function under the circumstances. In my work, I've encountered accident victims so battered and bloody, it could have been distracting or even disturbing, were I to dwell on it. With support devices in every orifice, it can be hard to imagine the patient as an intact person walking or driving around just a short time ago.

Sometimes, there is no representative to answer for a patient, and in true emergencies, we waive the usual consent process in order to act in the best interest of the patient right away. Other times, a distraught family is at the bedside, and I must concisely explain what I can offer. Communicating quickly in a sensitive manner is an incredibly important skill to master. Once the patient is positioned and prepped, I must focus on my role, and perform it as quickly as I can. Whether the patient gags on their endotracheal tube or the nurse fusses with the monitoring leads, I mustn't be distracted from my task: to find the bleeding vessel and shut it down.

As the blood pressure drops, it's a race against the clock, and my performance is enhanced by adrenaline. I'm not thinking of anything but the vessel I'm in and the next step forward. Once I embolize the culprit, I can relax a bit. The blood pressure stabilizes, and a sense of relief permeates the room. That's how fast the feedback from an intervention can be. And the feeling is unbeatable. Rising to a challenge makes me feel strong, and being able to stop the bleeding gives me a rush of satisfaction. And you will find the rush that drives you, too.

In fields like mine, sometimes life-threatening situations can arise without warning. The first patient I lost was a terminal cancer patient who needed a biliary drainage. Mass-effect from his tumor was preventing bile from draining from the liver into the bowel, and when I punctured his bile ducts to place a drainage tube, he became unresponsive; he became septic from the bacteria multiplying in his obstructed ducts. He did not want to be resuscitated, given his prognosis. Though the procedure was meant to be palliative, to improve the quality of his remaining days, unexpectedly, the complication cut them short. I ruminated over the incident, replaying the moment he stopped responding, and speculating about what I could have done differently. I should have temporarily reversed his "do not intubate" (DNI) order; maybe then he'd have survived. Despite the sudden loss, his wife was understanding, and I helped comfort her. When you grapple with death, sometimes you lose.

You won't be able to save everyone, but in your role, you will do an incredible amount of good. There are countless times I've delivered good news to a patient and their family. Other times, just knowing that we've tried has been enough to aid a grieving family. Even in the face of death, the bright moments outweigh the dark ones. The work is so gratifying that it fills my heart most days.

As fellow IR, Dr. Natosha Monfore put it, "Saving lives is the best part of my job. When patients do well, and cases go as planned-- or even if the case becomes complex but I have a good outcome-- I feel a sense of pride, even giddiness. After these cases, I do a little happy dance! My techs laugh at me. But it is *this* feeling that keeps me going on days when the IR gods aren't working in my favor, or when I have a bad outcome."

Doubts about the Life-Saving Lifestyle

Maybe you are willing to face life-threatening crises but aren't sure if doing so will allow for a life outside of the hospital. While some physicians view the decision to treat emergencies as a trade-off, I can attest that it's still possible to have a fulfilling life outside of the procedure suite. Whether it's worth the time and personal sacrifice to do this kind of work is wholly up to you.

In training, I knew my attendings had families, but we didn't talk about work-life balance per se. One attending woke early each morning to go fishing before work, as his wife helped the kids get ready for school. Another had two young daughters, and when asked if he'd encourage them to go into medicine one day, he'd reply, "No way. It's too hard." As a trainee, it was hard to relate to the snippets of attending life I heard about. Though they were role models in many ways, when I looked at my attendings, there was a disconnect when I tried to imagine what my future life would be like if I followed a similar path.

In the back of my mind, I wondered, would I have to marry a surgeon so he wouldn't be emasculated by my career? Would my future partner-- if I found one-- fill in the gaps that resulted from my long hours at the hospital? Would domestic expectations be higher for me as a woman? Would I live up to my roles as a mother and/or wife? Would my hypothetical family understand the struggles attendant to my chosen field? There were many unknowns, and without a female role model, I took a leap of faith. I didn't want to let the unknown lifestyle piece scare me away from the field I truly wanted to pursue.

My concerns were bolstered by some of the advice I received in residency. Several attendings seemed to discourage me from pursuing IR. They were the smartest people I'd ever known, so I listened to what they said about the demands of having a family and the stress of being on call. Historically, most of the women in my residency program went on to specialize in women's imaging. This subspecialty was encouraged as an option that allowed for predictable hours and an overall less demanding work life. But I didn't connect with the work or the patients I found there. If I had dedicated my career to the field, I don't think I would be nearly as satisfied in my career as I am now. That's why I feel strongly that each physician must choose her specialty based on the kind of work she would like to do. In my view, this is far more important than choosing based on subjective, variable, or malleable factors like lifestyle.

When I asked my friend and freshly-minted attending, Dr. Natosha Monfore, if she considered the on-call lifestyle to be a burden, she replied, "I actually enjoy being on call. While it can be stressful and anxiety-provoking, it is my time to shine. Being on call allows me to do a variety of cases that I don't typically get to do in my everyday practice. Often, these cases are challenging, forcing me to think outside of the box while doing the best I can to provide the patient with a positive outcome."

Several years into my career, I feel blessed to know many talented women in my field who feel the same way.

Can or Should Women Do Life-Saving Work?

When I was choosing a subspecialty, some seemed to assume I'd choose based on my demographic-- that I'd want to be where the other girls were. Besides, there seemed to be an assumption that women who wanted children should have no interest in taking emergency call. There were a few issues with that logic for me. First, I didn't have a partner, let alone a child at that time. And more importantly, those were not the factors I wanted to dictate my career choice. I did know that whatever my career looked like in the future, I wanted to have a life outside of the hospital. I wondered if it was possible to have a meaningful career as a physician without sacrificing all the enjoyment in my life. Despite the risks, I forged ahead, into my field of choice, and I'm so glad I did. So if you desire a career in a traditionally male-dominated field, don't let others' assumptions derail you.

Sometimes, other people's assumptions and biases can make for an exclusionary environment. Dr. Lola Oladini shared the feeling of being overlooked, particularly as a woman of color in her field: "As a URM (under-represented minority) woman pursuing IR, I sometimes jokingly debate with myself about which identity lends greater invisibility." As an example, she told me that one day, the Society of Interventional Radiology's social media campaign entitled, "#IamIR" came up for discussion. The campaign aimed to showcase and encourage increased diversity within the specialty, which includes only 9% women, and just 2% black physicians at the fellow and attending levels. Dr. Oladini recounted how: "In relation to the campaign, a senior resident commented, 'I don't know why they're making a big deal of this; IR is one of the most diverse fields in medicine-- it's mainly brown people and Asians.' And as the black woman in the room, I wondered-- where does that leave me? And then, to blend in, I chuckled and laughed right along with them."

In addition to this feeling of invisibility, women entering the traditionally male-dominated fields of medicine still experience sexism. It runs rampant in our culture, and the paternalistic world of medicine is no exception. Even in the hyper-educated post-graduate world, more training on egalitarianism and implicit bias is needed. One insidious type of sexism women may face is dubbed 'benevolent sexism.' This brand of sexism is fed by the notion that other people know what's best for you because you're a woman. Too often, advice injected with benevolent sexism encourages women to limit themselves, often instilling fear in the process. If your inner alarm bells alert you to the potential that sexism may be at play, try asking: Would they be saying this if I were a man? If the answer is no, you might consider the comment or advice to be suspect. Yet even in modern times, women are making decisions based in part on this kind of guidance. That's why it's become my mission to spread awareness around the issue, through my blog, and in this book.

Being Taken Seriously

While some women feel discouraged from pursuing their field of choice, others can find it hard to be taken seriously once they're in practice. This is not to dissuade you from these career paths, but to arm you with the knowledge that this dynamic persists. It's important to note that if you encounter this kind of sexism, it doesn't mean anything about your capabilities as a physician.

Dr. Susan O'Horo, an academic IR in the Northeast confided, "It can be difficult as a female, particularly as one who is short and blonde, to be taken seriously in a male-dominated specialty. That's why I feel more at liberty to talk about my kids with my 'mommy friends' than I do at work-- most of the guys at work don't discuss their home lives. I think women have to be careful not to get placed on a "mommy track." The more you talk about your kids and home life, the more some people will assume you're not serious about your career. This could result in being passed over for opportunities. But I think this is less of an issue for your generation, which is more aware of the value of authenticity and integration of all aspects of one's life."

This is a fair warning from an experienced physician who has worked at various academic institutions: know your audience. If you're not in a particularly progressive setting, you may opt to share less of your personal life at work. You can use how much your colleagues share as a gauge, or simply do what makes you most comfortable.

What Do You Really Want From Your Career?

As a radiology resident, I mustered the courage to share my plan to pursue a career in IR with one of my 'nice' attendings. He balked: "You want to do IR? Yeah right!" A short time later, a more junior attending, Dr. Prince took me out for a sandwich. I'll always remember that day, in which we sat outside discussing my future. Outside of the hospital, I felt other people's opinions fall away. As we enjoyed our food, I shared my concerns and doubts about the future. He told me that I could in fact become an IR if I wanted to. Neither of us realized the gravity of our conversation that day, but years later, I told him the impact it had had on me, giving me the reassurance I needed to pursue my goals in earnest. "Thanks for the career," I said, in a half-joking tone, to lighten the weighty statement. "I owe it to you." I could tell he was taken aback, as he responded, "...You're welcome!" While I was ultimately the one responsible for my success, he'd given me permission to succeed.

I'm grateful that with some soul-searching and the right counsel, I gathered the confidence to declare my path and pursue it. I was intimidated by my chosen field, and the prospect of being responsible for the sickest patients under my care, but in the end, the desire to save lives overshadowed my fears. I wanted to not only diagnose a tumor in the liver but to treat it myself. I knew I could be the one to not only see where a patient was bleeding on a CT scan but the one who also strategically shut the bleeder down. Despite the narrative surrounding the surgical lifestyle, I followed my inner compass and became an interventional radiologist. Several years later, I'm living proof that you can save lives and still enjoy your own. I love the life I've created, and it's been a joy to witness my female colleagues in surgically-oriented fields do the same as well. I encourage you to create the life you want, no matter what others may say.

Spill Your Guts

🙂 Have you ever witnessed any situations in which a life was saved due to the advances of medicine or the heroism of a doctor?
  - How did that make you feel?
  - Can you imagine yourself in their shoes?

🙂 Have you ever witnessed a patient die?
  - How did that make you feel?
  - What were some things the healthcare team did to allow for dignity in the process and/ or to support the surviving family members?

🙂 What were some key moments or comments that have instilled doubt, or undercut your confidence in the pursuit of your career goals?

▫ When you examine the source or content, can you dismantle or dismiss them? For example, is it possible the offender didn't know you well or misjudged you somehow?

🦾 Start a professional brag sheet. On my blog, I explain how to use a curated list of accomplishments & compliments to boost your confidence.

▫ Head to https://tiredsuperheroine.com/try-a-brag-sheet-to-boost-your-career/ to read the post, including some of my own examples.

CHAPTER 5

Welcome to Challenge

While saving a life as a physician is incredible, it's not an easy path. Becoming a doctor requires a prolonged effort, requiring consistency, discipline, and grit. It involves years of intense study and memorization, the likes of which you may have never seen before. It involves skipped meals and the Socratic Method, a teaching method in which students are put on the spot to answer difficult questions, often in a group setting. With your fellow aspiring doctors, you'll cram together into shared living spaces and lecture halls. You'll spend years on a single-minded schedule consisting of study, eat, study, re-caffeinate, study, sleep, and repeat. As a student, I learned to meet my needs for food, the bathroom, or coffee as efficiently as possible, so I could get back to studying. In a seemingly perpetual cycle, my classmates and I focused on that next test score or next clerkship grade.

As you stretch yourself mentally and physically, you'll be learning an entirely new language, comprising anatomy, microbiology, pharmacology, and more. And the pace of learning doesn't slow down once you graduate from medical school. In training, you'll learn the art and lexicon of your chosen specialty. It's a massive undertaking, but if you're still reading this book, I know you're up to the task.

As you confront these challenges, they will help bond you to your fellow students. Together, you'll experience the sacrifices of becoming a physician. While your college friends transition from partying to starting their careers, buying new homes, and having kids, you'll be studying medicine. I spent a thousand days and nights burrowed in a cubicle. Occasionally I'd look up from my books to rest my eyes, watch a passerby, and momentarily remember that people in the outside world were doing other things. Then I'd return to my text or study guide and get back to work. During those years, I studied in book shops and parks, on buses and trains. This is the kind of dedication you'll need.

This Challenge Will Help You Grow-- Fast

Beyond the steep learning curve of training, practicing as an attending is challenging too. Patients are sicker than they've ever been, as they live longer and accumulate comorbidities. Beyond their complexity, sick people can be difficult, and it can take an emotional toll.

Recently, I had a patient with peritoneal carcinomatosis, who was extremely uncomfortable. A gynecologic malignancy had spread to stud and coat the lining of her abdomen, as it filled with fluid, compressing her organs and bowel. This process can even cause bowel obstruction. I proposed an ultrasound-guided paracentesis to remove some of the fluid from her abdomen, with the aim of relieving some discomfort. This normally straightforward procedure became difficult as she was obese, and we couldn't see much aside from her solid pelvic masses. I couldn't seem to find a window to place my centesis needle. During this process, she complained the entire time. Finally, she refused the procedure and went for a follow-up CT (computed tomography) scan. To our surprise, it showed massive free air, likely a rupture of her previously distended colon.

I was relieved I hadn't attempted a procedure on her, lest I be blamed for causing her intestinal perforation. The incident reminded me that no matter how challenging patients can be, we must maintain the utmost professionalism and do our best. If I'd gotten flustered or been hasty, I could have made a mistake or attempted a procedure of marginal safety. Paradoxically, the encounter left me feeling grateful. Taking care of the sickest patients is a gift, which has provided me an impetus to grow as a physician, time and again. Situations like these push me to communicate better, be more compassionate, and hone my skills every day.

That said, daily encounters with sick patients can lead to emotional fatigue, even exhaustion, for some healthcare workers. For some patients, it's possible that nothing you do could possibly alleviate their suffering, let alone make them happy with your care. As physicians, we must realize that the patients we see may be going through some of the toughest moments of their lives. Beyond maintaining an awareness of the stresses involved in such work, we must take care of ourselves intentionally, taking the time we need to recharge, complete life-maintenance activities, and simply rest. These are simple ways in which you can "refill your cup" as a physician. Despite the sometimes blistering pace of training, it's important to create a sustainable schedule once you become an attending. Otherwise, it can be easy to get overwhelmed by clinical demands.

The Challenge Bonds You to Your Family in Medicine

One of the upsides of the challenges in medicine is the camaraderie that often comes with them. Because members of your specialty share many of the same joys and pitfalls as you do, they can understand you in a way others simply can't. When I curse under my breath, securing a difficult access in a tortuous vessel, my first-assist is right there with me, sharing the pleasure and the pain. When your team completes a complex case with the help of seamless communication, you might feel as though you're part of a force larger than yourself. On the other hand, when a delay in patient transport means the whole team goes home late, you share in the frustration.

In reality, the stressors in medicine extend beyond the threat of disease or complication, to include increasing administrative oversight, decreased autonomy, and political and financial challenges. As you face these obstacles together, the relationships with your medical family members grow and develop.

Dr. Annie Gill shares her own experience of bonding with her work family: "Challenging cases, patients, and life circumstances have bonded me to my people in medicine. This includes technologists, schedulers, nurses, and of course, my fellow physicians. I feel supported by a truly wonderful team that is more like family than friends. We always watch out for one another and try to give consistent answers to questions or consults, in order to provide one another with support. We celebrate wins together and cry together when things do not go as we'd hoped. This group did not come together quickly nor by chance; it was carefully chosen. The relationships have developed over time and through our experiences together."

Balancing Work with Life Outside of the Hospital

Now, more than ever, doctors seek fulfillment outside of their careers. They no longer expect to live in the hospital or become martyrs to their profession, as physicians of the past did. Whether this means the freedom to socialize with friends regularly, start a family, or both, this balance may look a little different for everyone. While you can't focus on or have everything under the sun, you will have plenty of options available to you as a physician. Many women entering medicine wonder whether it is possible to balance a surgically-oriented career with a life outside of the hospital. In my experience, it can be done, with some planning and a little creativity. Even when an overall balance is achieved, there will still be moments or even seasons of imbalance, and that's okay. As you find and maintain your own personal balance, it's important to remember that you always have choices.

I'll give an example of a time I chose to "do it all." One night, when my son was 19 months old, I was on call for the local medical center. I finished my work early enough to attend a staff meeting for another hospital in our network, which was scheduled thirty minutes away. As I planned my evening, I remembered that I hadn't yet seen my little boy, and I missed him. When I arrived home, my husband was sprawled on the bed, wiped out from a day of solo-parenting. He was too tired to accompany me to the dinner event that followed my staff meeting. Quickly weighing my options, I decided to bring my boy along.

Armed with a banana and a sippy cup, I arrived at the meeting ten minutes late, maneuvering my umbrella stroller to an empty aisle seat. As the director of the emergency department briefed us on quarterly volumes, my toddler munched lumps of fruit, craning to see the speaker. I even provided an impromptu update for my department, despite having banana slime on my hands. My little boy and I made it through the meeting without any disruption, and I felt triumphant. That night, I got to be a doctor and a mom at the same time.

Doing It All, Partnership, and Getting Help

In general, I rely on built-in help, from my husband or from someone else, so I don't have to do so much multitasking. But from time to time, you might consider doing it all, just because you can. I could have skipped that meeting, but I chose to attend, with my son and I both benefiting from the experience. And while this approach wouldn't work with a colicky infant or a disruptive toddler, that day, I got to experience the accomplishment of balancing my roles.

As an attending, you'll have ample resources to deploy when you need them. For example, my husband and I have a part-time nanny to help us with childcare and basic household tasks. I speak more about how my family approaches parenting and running a two-career household on my blog at TiredSuperheroine.com. Suffice it to say, with the right planning in place, you shouldn't routinely feel like you need to do it all. There are many ways to cultivate a personal and/ or family balance. Countless working parents in medicine have come before for us. Those with different family structures and with fewer resources have figured out how to make it work, and you will too.

For me, finding a supportive partner has been an invaluable way to enrich my life outside of the hospital. If you want to have a family in a surgical or procedural career, having a true partner can be key to making it work. Despite my misgivings about dating in medical school, I eventually found someone who wasn't emasculated by my work titles and was proud of my ability to save lives. When we met, he didn't know what it meant to be a resident, so he didn't grasp the fact that I was a doctor. Over time, he witnessed my dedication to my career and decided to follow me across the country to pursue a prestigious fellowship. That year, he stood by me, never knowing when I'd be home, but understanding I'd be at the hospital until the work was done. He cooked for me and coped with the erratic schedule.

As a musician and music teacher, my husband has a less demanding and more flexible schedule than mine. He often serves as the primary parent to our toddler. He doesn't "help" me with the housework, but takes ownership of his share. And while our relationship is not perfect, we have a true partnership at home. Some women who operate have a stay at home spouse, while others are part of a dual-physician family. Each structure will have its own dynamic, depending on the number of careers at play and how flexible they are. In my experience, finding the best strategies to accommodate a two-career household is an ongoing process.

As Theresa Caridi, MD, FSIR explains, "At times I've doubted my career choice for personal reasons: Why couldn't I have chosen something with more flexibility, where I could work from anywhere? Ultimately, I found that while there might not be inherent flexibility in my work, I can control many of my circumstances with a deliberate effort. For example, I can choose to surround myself with a strong group of individuals who have common goals and ethics. I can choose how I react to, process, and internalize what happens around me (although admittedly, this always needs improvement!). It's my choice to prioritize my family and relationships. Finding what suits you best is a process of trial and error."

Spill Your Guts

- What are some challenges you've faced as a student or trainee that have ultimately brought you closer to your colleagues?

- What concerns do you have around work-life balance as you become a proceduralist or surgeon?
  - Brainstorm some possible solutions to these challenges.

- What is important to you outside of medicine?
  - How will you make space for those things or people in your life?

- What are some ways in which you manage stress?
  - How do you take care of yourself?
  - When you feel exhausted, what kinds of activities replenish you?
  - What are some resources you could use to learn more ways to manage stress?

CHAPTER 6

Nix the Naysayers

As I alluded to earlier, once I had decided on my sub-specialty, I waited before telling others in my residency program. I think it's because, in a way, I felt unworthy. I doubted myself as a budding IR and was afraid of what others would say. It felt like I had to be absolutely certain about my choice before I could share it with others. I secretly wondered:

> Would people think I was smart enough to be an IR?
> Would people laugh at me when I told them my plans?
> Would they feel sorry for me, thinking I'd never fit in or be respected in my field?

If this sounds familiar, maybe you are doubting yourself or stalling in sharing your aspirations with others. But expressing interest in your field is key to learning as much as you can during medical school and training. Not only that, but it's also integral to building the support system you'll need in order to apply for the program or position you desire. In waiting, you put yourself at a disadvantage compared to those who declare their interests sooner. Though I may have indulged in self-doubt longer than I should have, I don't entirely blame myself. That's because even today, women who operate still encounter paternalistic and out-dated ideas in medicine. Even in the 2020s, female trainees are told, "You can't practice/ match into/ succeed in (insert competitive/ male-dominated field) if you're female."

Maybe you find this statement preposterous. Or perhaps you've heard some version of it yourself. The truth is, procedural fields like IR and surgery are about deft hands, good judgment, and working well under pressure-- not about your gender. Succeeding in these fields doesn't depend on the length of your hair, the color of your skin, or the god(s) you bow to. It just doesn't.

Don't Be Surprised If You Encounter These Myths

A common myth I encounter is that the surgically-oriented fields are too physical for women. And while it's true that they can require standing for long periods of time, women have done this for eons. I may stand for one to three hours during a complex limb revascularization case. Compare that to your teachers growing up who stood all day-- I'm guessing were predominantly female. It's true that during some kinds of surgery, a lead (or equivalent) apron can add weight and potential strain on the body. That's why it's important that this garment fits properly, regardless of your size or dimensions. This helps to avoid associated musculoskeletal problems like back pain. The problem is, as students and residents rotate through and "try on" the specialty, there may not be an appropriately sized garment to borrow, especially if they are petite-- leaving them with an ill-fitting apron-- and clinical experience. In addition to properly fitted "lead," good ergonomics and core strength can help prevent physical strain in men and women alike.

Another common myth is that radiation is bad for women. My field and others like it use fluoroscopy, or live x-ray, to help navigate through the body. Unfortunately, misinformation and fear about radiation can deter interested women from procedural fields like mine. Although a full discussion of radiation safety is beyond the scope of this book, suffice it to say that women have operated in this way for decades, without deleterious effects to themselves or their children. The SIR's online Pregnancy Toolkit contains resources including safety data, best practices for radiation protection, and post-partum resources, too. It can be found at https://www.sirweb.org/practice-resources/toolkits/pregnancy-toolkit/.

Other fields that commonly use fluoroscopy include interventional cardiology, vascular surgery, and orthopaedics, for example. Operators in these fields wear radiation protection in all cases where fluoro is used. When the usual precautions are taken, the dose to the fetus of a pregnant woman can be so low as to be undetectable. In reality, everyone working with fluoroscopy benefits from taking appropriate precautions, using protective equipment, and keeping the radiation dose as low as reasonably achievable (ALARA).

Elitism

Other misconceptions about the procedural fields center around the competitiveness of securing a training position. I've still heard the idea circulating that students shouldn't pursue certain specialties if they are an immigrant, or if they are not from a physician family. However, many physicians in competitive fields are immigrants. I am a daughter of Eastern European immigrants and the first American doctor in my family. Dr. Josef Rosch, who pioneered the TIPS (transjugular intrahepatic portosystemic shunt) procedure was a Czech immigrant. He left an indelible mark through his work at the famed Dotter Institute, the birthplace of IR. Our field and others like it are built in part on the sweat and ingenuity of people like him.

As an Armenian immigrant coming from a Caribbean medical school, Dr. Anna Gasparyan faced similar attitudes on the road to becoming a vascular surgeon. As a student, she was told,

"No one will ever take you seriously. You will never become a surgeon." Despite the put-downs, she pressed on. During her surgical residency, she became interested in vascular surgery. But because of her low in-service exam scores, she says, the chair of the department discouraged her: "Be satisfied that you'll be a general surgeon. You don't need to do a fellowship. Vascular surgery is not for ladies." In spite of his remarks, Dr. Gasparyan found support in her Program Director, a fellowship-trained colorectal surgeon. "She was very supportive and said, 'If you want it, go for it.'"

Sifting Through 'Advice'

Sometimes, discouraging words can be more subtle, masquerading as advice. Hannah Clode, a third-year medical student is still affected by an episode that occurred the first time she entered the procedure suite. She recounts, "I was completely doe-eyed, caught up in the hustle and bustle of what was happening. It was awesome. I was asking everyone questions-- not just the residents and attendings, but the techs and ancillary staff, too. Everyone has an interesting take on what's going on. Long story short, I got some advice that IR really isn't what I want to do. That it's a lot of work, and it's tiring." Unsure how to process this comment, she brushed it off at the time. But she continued, "Whenever I see that person, he still asks, 'You still want to do IR?' in an incredulous tone as if to imply, 'I warned you.' And that has stuck with me." She went on to doubt her own perceptions, saying, "Maybe I'm too impressionable, or maybe this person has a point. He's been an IR for maybe 20 years... It's hard to know who to trust, or how much to take stock of other people's perspectives."

When examining the comments through the lens of potential sexism, she reflected: "It's hard to say if he'd say that if I were a man. I feel like maybe he still might have. He's an ex-marine and he's cool. He'd teach me stuff on the back table without me asking. Maybe that's why our conversation that day stuck with me-- because he was one of the few people who introduced himself and didn't turf me to the side. It seemed like he cared. But also, he was like, 'IR is busy and hard. Do something else. Something like anesthesia. Now that's a great career.'"

Personally, I've witnessed this "grass is greener" attitude among seasoned docs from time to time. A number of factors can underlie this attitude, a common one being burnout. It's possible the physician in Hannah's story feels trapped in the wrong job or hasn't found the right personal balance. But in projecting his woes on Hannah, he leaves her confused and questioning the future. In reflecting on the dilemma presented by his comments, she explains, "I'm not afraid of hard. I am afraid of unhappiness." When thinking through your own career choices, it's important to realize that no job or specialty can determine your happiness on its own. Many other variables will contribute. And the particular issues or challenges faced by one attending don't necessarily have any bearing on you or your future. So be aware of this phenomenon, and remember, unhappy attendings can unwittingly project their baggage onto you.

With an impressive degree of insight, Hannah expresses what we are all afraid of. And her statement gets at the heart of the matter for many female trainees. Sometimes, they must scrutinize the advice they receive, and discard it if it doesn't seem to fit. Teasing apart the advice you receive can take extra bandwidth. But separating useful advice from the unuseful is a worthwhile skill to learn.

I recall personally ruminating over an unhelpful, unsolicited opinion, as I prepared for my first Ironman triathlon. Completing an Ironman was a dream of mine since childhood when my Dad and I would watch it together on TV. Like the challenge of becoming a doctor, I saw the Ironman as a way to train myself to be the best I could be, and test my limits. The race and the people who attempted it inspired me, and I wanted to see if I could complete the 2.4-mile swim, 112-mile bike course, and 26.2-mile marathon myself. Several months into training, an out of shape co-worker told me I had no business doing an Ironman, and that it should be reserved for elite athletes. I was taken aback at his discouragement-- why did he even care what I did, or whether I belonged in the race or not? Using his rebuke as fuel, I plowed through the final months of training and relished my accomplishment at the finish line. It was one of the best days of my life, and I'm so glad I didn't let his opinions get in the way.

Like training for an Ironman, becoming a proceduralist or surgeon can be grueling, mentally, and physically. Some of us pursue these careers not in spite of the fact that they're demanding, but in part because of the challenge involved. And if you're like Dr. Agnes Solberg, an IR in North Dakota, the rebel in you may even be encouraged by a naysayer's words. She shared, "Since I was a little girl, I have wanted to accomplish things that I wasn't allowed to do, was told I could not do, or that were for boys. So instead of tennis, I played rugby. I learned to snowboard before it was cool for girls. I joined the Army."

On top of the inherent difficulties of becoming a woman who operates, some may try to dissuade you or tell you you don't belong. So if you know you want to practice in a male-dominated field, prepare to dismiss some naysayers along the way. You can learn to dodge their misguided advice and strengthen your inner voice enough to drown them out.

Spill Your Guts

🔖 Have you ever had to deal with a naysayer in your past?
  - How did you handle it? What was the outcome?

🔖 Do you feel worthy of choosing a medical career based on your desires and talents?
  - Why or why not?

🔖 What obstacles do you foresee in your path in medicine?
  - How do you think you'll approach these obstacles?
  - Who can you call on for help?

CHAPTER 7

Confronting Doubt: Do I Belong Here?

In medical training, doubt can come with the territory. It's normal to wonder if you're good enough, as you're learning as fast as you possibly can. But sometimes, being in a competitive, male-dominated environment can amplify doubt even further. In my diagnostic radiology program, there were seven residents per class, and of those, only one or two females were selected each year. Radiology is a male-dominated specialty, so I was surrounded by men, most of the time. And there was an undercurrent of competition, which came to feel like a sibling rivalry. Each of us was always trying to prove him or herself, and jockey for the attendings' favor. Personally, there were weeks and months that I wondered whether I was the dumbest one in my class. As I struggled to compete with the guys (and other girl) in my class, those four years grew long.

Theresa Carridi, MD, FSIR, reflected on her own doubts as a trainee, including the gender bias she'd internalized. "I have nearly always felt accepted by my male colleagues as an attending. But during training, this was not always the case. Now, I think my feeling accepted is probably in large part due to my gaining confidence that I, as a female, add value to the team-- it took a while to believe this myself."

Beyond the implicit biases that persist, some women are told they simply don't belong in certain fields. "Throughout my journey, I was persistently discouraged," said Dr. Anna Gasparyan, a vascular surgeon in my community. "You're female; you need to get married and have kids. Surgery is not for you," she recounted of the comments she received. Overall, training is tough, and it can be further complicated by being in the minority in a male-dominated field. Despite the added challenges, you have the power to excel despite the doubts that may cross your mind. Having mentors and advisors to help remind you of this when you forget is incredibly valuable.

Where Are the Women?

When I decided to pursue my subspecialty, I was moving from the male-dominated field of diagnostic radiology to the even *more* male-dominated field of interventional radiology. While 23% of diagnostic radiologists are female, only 9% of practicing IRs are. And a skewed demographic is also seen in many of the procedurally-oriented sub-specialties of medicine. Some are listed in the table below, along with some primary care specialties for comparison.

Table 1. Percentage of Active Physicians by Sex and Specialty, from AAMC 2017

Specialty	Percentage of practicing physicians who are female
Pediatrics	63.3
OB/GYN	57
All Medical Specialties	35.2
Critical Care Medicine	26.1
Diagnostic Radiology	25.6
General Surgery	20.6
Gastroenterology	17.6
Vascular Surgery	13.1
Interventional Radiology	9.5
Urology	8.7
Neurological Surgery	8.4
Interventional Cardiology	7.7
Orthopaedic Surgery	5.3

As you can see from the data above, if you feel like the odd woman out in your specialty, you probably are. In some male-dominated fields, a boys' club atmosphere can feel exclusionary, as the guys chat about sports, or the drinks you weren't invited to last night. Some women may be put-off or deterred by the "locker room" vibe inherent to certain fields.

When I arrived in IR each morning as a resident, it felt like entering an actual men's locker room. There were men's shoes, men's jackets, men's bags, and men's lead aprons... everywhere. I would quickly put aside the thought, place my things among them, and get to work. And while the atmosphere wasn't overtly unwelcoming, it felt a little unfamiliar. That's why as an attending who encourages other women to join our ranks, I'm concerned that when a female student or trainee enters this kind of space, the foreignness can be enough to plant a seed of doubt about whether she belongs or is welcome there.

As a resident rotating through my future field, the fellows were generally nice to me and treated me as part of the team. In morning report, we were "pimped" together, answering questions on vascular anatomy and procedural techniques. It was intimidating to learn this way, but it kept me on my toes. Knowing I'd be put on the spot kept me motivated to study. I couldn't wait to grow up and be like the fellows I looked up to so much. But every day, doubt lurked in the back of my mind: did I belong in this subspecialty, or was I just passing through?

Nancy Yen Shipley, MD reflected on her own experience entering the boys' club of orthopaedic surgery. "Every once in a while, I'd look around and think, 'Huh... I'm the only female here.' And to me, it was almost an afterthought. It wasn't until much later, as I rotated through some sub-internships that I witnessed true unconscious bias on the part of one of the residents. He was extremely nice, but he just never really taught me much. Then he would turn to a new med student and start teaching him all these fracture classifications," she said. "And I realized that it had only to do with the fact that I was female. I think he just didn't know how to teach or talk to a woman. To this day, I don't think he meant anything by it, and that he probably would've been surprised if I brought it up to him."

As NancyMD points out, unconscious bias can be sneaky, often escaping unrecognized by its perpetrator and its victims. But regardless of the intention behind them, incidents like these can become frustrating and discouraging for those affected. Importantly, Dr. Yen Shipley didn't blame herself for her resident's shortcomings. For those who are open to improving upon their biases, moments like these can serve as learning opportunities. Identifying and correcting this kind of behavior is especially important in those responsible for teaching you, the next generation of physicians.

Refocus Your Attention

If you find the demographics of your chosen field is tripping you up, making you second-guess your interest, consider shifting your attention. Instead of focusing on how you're different from the people around you, focus on the work itself, and on the patient population you serve. This is easier said than done sometimes, and it's completely understandable to feel like the odd woman out in a male-dominated field. But by re-focusing your attention, you can get a more accurate view of how you might fit in within your chosen specialty. For example, if you truly don't like the sight of blood, I doubt you'd still be reading this book, and in that case, the procedural fields might not be for you. On the other hand, if you dream of doing stealthy image-guided procedures or elegant laparoscopic surgeries, that matters far more than the fact that your field is currently lacking in diversity.

Dr. Lola Oladini shared her experience with self-doubt, and the strategies she's used to overcome it. "At multiple junctures in my life, I've either struggled with imposter syndrome, self-doubt, or someone else telling me I wouldn't succeed. In college and med school, I felt like I was "faking it." But I decided that ultimately, it doesn't matter how I get there, how long it takes me, or how hard it is for me relative to the next gal, as long as I get there too. I try my best to redirect my focus from whether or not I belong, to what I can do while I'm there. This greater sense of purpose transcends any self-doubt I may feel."

Micro-Cultures and Local Environments

It's important to note that even within a given specialty, no two environments are exactly alike. The procedure suites and operating rooms you ultimately work in may not resemble or feel like that of your training institutions; countless variables will contribute to your environment once you are out in practice. These factors may be regional, institutional, or interpersonal. Ultimately, the particular setting and practice you choose to work in will be up to you.

To give you an example, I spent four years in New England, during my diagnostic radiology residency. There, I endured seemingly endless side conversations about professional sports which made my eyes glaze over. Often, I was the only woman in the room. And when I wasn't, the other woman present could usually hold her own in these conversations much better than I could. Aside from being smart and hard-working, talking sports was the easiest way to connect with the attendings and be seen as part of the team. Enthusiasm for New England sports was practically a requirement to be selected Chief Resident.

When I relocated to Los Angeles for fellowship, there wasn't nearly as much emphasis on sports. I'd entered a new culture, where even the way we handled consults felt completely different. Now that I practice in the Southern California desert, the conversations tend to center around co-workers' kids, electric vehicles, and local cultural events. Experiences in different places have shown me a wide array of micro-cultures, even within the fields of diagnostic and interventional radiology. And some have felt more inclusive than others.

I asked Dr. Susan O'Horo if she ever felt like the odd woman out, during training or beyond. "All the time!" She responded. "I am often the only female physician in the room, particularly in radiology or IR meetings. Not to say there are *no* women in radiology, but there are far fewer compared to other specialties. But this seems to be improving. The private practice I am joining has quite a few female physicians in leadership, including at the highest levels. I am really looking forward to that experience."

I asked Aneesa Majid, MD, MBA if she has ever felt like the odd woman out in her career. "The simple answer is yes," she began. "My whole career, actually." When I asked her how this has affected her career trajectory, she replied, "Sometimes ignorance is bliss. I didn't really realize how male-dominated IR was when I started. It wasn't until I began working in private practice that I witnessed the obstacles of being a woman in a male-dominated sphere first-hand, particularly as the only female within a practice. It was such a problem in my first practice that it spurred me to leave. However, this set me on a course into leadership, to learn more about how unconscious bias affects organizations and culture. My early experiences helped to strengthen my voice both for myself and others. Now, I use that voice to help other women, and to mentor those who are coming up through the ranks."

As you search for the optimal practice, rest assured that there are places where women can not only fit in but fulfill their greatest potential. If you aspire to become a leader in your career but are not in a practice that supports women in these roles, it might be time to move on and find one that does, as Drs. Majid and O'Horo have.

Is it Possible to Stand Out in a Good Way?

As a woman pursuing a procedural path, you may feel self-conscious about standing out in a male-dominated field. As I've described, this can foster self-doubt or a sense of other-ness. But did you ever consider that standing out could actually be an asset? On fellowship interviews, I stood out from the crowd, as a woman in a sea of men. As the only female candidate at most of my interviews, I felt a certain "leg-up" on the competition, if for nothing else than for being different, and therefore, memorable. Being memorable is key to getting ranked in the residency and fellowship selection process. And while interview skills and a strong application are integral to your success, simply standing out can make a difference. I'm proof of it.

Dr. Lola Oladini attests that it's possible to turn a perceived liability into a strength. "As a woman in a profession dominated by men, I am very cautious not to come across as "too aggressive." Somewhat unexpectedly, this has helped make me a better listener in group settings. Often, it has helped me see a strategy that I may have otherwise overlooked if I'd felt comfortable enough to jump in without listening first." Hers is an example of how a personal strength, the ability to synthesize information to formulate a strategy, is enhanced by the fact that she doesn't force herself to conform to the behavior of her male peers. Now *that's* standing out in a good way.

Spill Your Guts

- How do you respond to competition?
  - Do you shrink from it, or thrive on it?
  - How do you think that has affected your career trajectory so far?
- Does the diversity of a specialty (or lack thereof) affect your approach to choosing your career?
  - Why or why not?
- In what ways can you stand out from the crowd, in order to gain a competitive advantage?
  - Name a few things that make you unique, even if they're not traditionally viewed as strengths.

CHAPTER 8

Your Specialty Needs Leaders

O nce you've settled into your chosen field, you might consider leading it. Your practice, your hospital, and your community need leaders like you to step forward. And even if you don't see yourself as a leader, you are. As a physician, you will be the de facto leader of a medical team. Whether you take on the challenges that exist beyond your individual scope of practice is a choice. The degree to which you incorporate leadership in the context of your career is up to you.

Motivated to Lead

Dr. Laura Findeiss, Past President of the Society of Interventional Radiology, is also a prominent leader at her own institution, as a Professor of Radiology and Surgery at the Emory University

School of Medicine. But she never considered herself to have leadership potential, in so many words. "Early on, I didn't think a lot about leading people, but more about fixing problems that I saw in the system. I needed to learn that the people part was critical to achieving success! I didn't aspire to leadership positions as much as I wanted to position myself to have influence over processes. There are so many dysfunctions in healthcare delivery systems that lend themselves to incremental improvement. If one is willing to take on these challenges, there is a natural progression towards ending up in a leadership position. In this way, growing into leadership is an extension of a passion for improvement. Better delivery of patient care has always been a real focus of my energy, and that focus has led the way."

It's clear to see why she has risen into leadership at a competitive academic center. Early in my career, I've likewise felt the drive to improve patient care, albeit in a different setting. In private practice in a small desert community, I've been asked to lead from an early point in my career, sometimes when a leadership void presented itself. In my first job out of training, the physician leading our section was drawn to work in another county, where he could be closer to his family. As a result, I was left to manage the service at a sizable medical center, largely on my own. During that time, I worked to build my reputation and further develop the service lines he'd established. That's why, when the time came to handoff section leadership, I was the obvious choice. I became Chief of Interventional Radiology, fresh off maternity leave, no less.

Falling Into Leadership

Later, when the Vice-Chair of our Radiology Department left the practice, a leadership void presented again, and I stepped into that role. Sometimes, if you're in the right place at the right time, you will be asked to lead. And if you're like me, sometimes, you'll feel out of your depth. If you're sort of "green" like I was, you may not even know what a particular role entails. It's okay to ask questions about the responsibilities of a post, and the time commitment involved. When I've taken a new leadership role, I've had a low threshold to call on more experienced colleagues for advice when I need to. These positions don't tend to come with an instruction manual, so I've learned by doing them and you can, too.

"But wait!" You may protest. I'm...

- too junior
- just a few years out of training
- afraid the staff/ partners/ administrators won't listen to me

I also faced these concerns as I took the helm. There is a learning curve to leading at any level, just as there is in the practice of medicine. If you can learn to perform an angiogram or remove a gallbladder, I'm confident you can learn nearly anything. And, learning to lead is no exception.

So what does leading in medicine mean? As a physician, leading is inherent to the work you perform daily. This kind of work involves constant communication and fielding patient-related and non-patient-related challenges every day. The foundation of my leadership skill lies in leading by example. I do this by maintaining a high standard for myself and others. When you consistently act in the best interest of the patient, you'll build a solid reputation. As you produce consistent quality work, everyone in the hospital will come to know it. This is powerful.

As a budding leader, aim to learn about your environment before trying to change it. When my practice hired a new physician, he was eager to change a number of processes, without taking the time to familiarize himself with the way things were currently done. Hasty changes can be disruptive or even harmful if they are undertaken without a baseline understanding of the systems and processes in place. And don't worry if you make mistakes along the way. You don't have to be perfect to be a leader. I'm proof.

Origins of a Leader

In fact, overcoming imperfect origins can be a strong foundation for leadership, as Dr. Findeiss describes: "As a kid, I was very shy, preferring to hang back and watch. No one would have pegged me as a future leader! We moved around a lot, so I was always adapting to new environments and people. I think that made me more comfortable with change and with not always being popular. This helped me to solidify my own values system and cling to that, rather than to the transient benefits of superficial friendships. As a leader, I think it's important to be comfortable with not always being liked, and that takes training."

In its early stages, exercising leadership can be as simple as identifying a problem and making moves to solve it. Whether your initial leadership roles involve a title or not, they can come with some growing pains. A couple of years into my role as an attending, I was working with a very experienced technologist. He was a former combat medic in the military before I was even born. Despite the discrepancy in age and rank, we worked together very well. One day, however, I noticed a discrepancy in the way the fluoroscopy (fluoro) times were noted on our paperwork. While one of the procedure suites provided fluoro time in tenths of a minute, the other provided the data in minutes and seconds. I realized we'd been reporting the fluoro times incorrectly in one of the suites for quite some time. Documenting the amount of x-ray time for each procedure is a regulatory mandate, and while this mistake wouldn't actually harm any patients-- the differences in reported times were a fraction of a minute-- we had clearly been documenting incorrectly for over a year.

I told the technologist my concern, but he didn't seem to understand. He'd been doing it that way for so long, and here was this new doctor telling him it was wrong. I reiterated the problem, in an attempt to clarify the issue. Later, his manager informed me that I'd upset him. Maybe he felt ashamed for making the error, or for not understanding what I was saying right away. Perhaps I was too forceful, concerned about my fluoroscopy license, as well as those of the other physicians in the department. And in my view, it seemed like a black and white issue: we needed to fix the way we documented fluoro times moving forward. As to past errors, the administration would have to decide what to do about them. As I flailed in my attempts to correct the problem, it became a bigger issue.

Bewildered, I asked my department chair for advice and was surprised by his response. When I explained the problem and the subsequent interaction, I asked what he would have done, expecting him to agree with my approach. He told me that after the tech didn't understand, he would have called the radiation physicist to deal with it. I was flabbergasted; in my mind, we were talking about a colon instead of a decimal point.

Why would I need a physicist to explain that? Surely I could deal with this myself, I thought.

Over time, the rough edges of the incident smoothed over, and the relationship was repaired. But my chair's political advice stuck with me. The straightforward, confrontational method doesn't always work, even if I think it should. With decades more experience than me, my chair was probably right. I still struggle with this non-linear approach, but that's okay. Leadership is a journey, and sometimes, it can get messy. Even when it does, know that you're learning and helping your institution and your patients in the process.

Maybe you're ready to try your hand at leadership, but don't see much in the way of opportunity. Consider whether you need to let your interest be known to the right individual or individuals, so they'll consider you when a position opens. In some practices, you might not be considered for a leadership position until several others retire. The competition for leadership positions can vary considerably. So if opportunities to lead are lacking at your institution, consider other venues to gain experience, like your state or national medical societies, for example.

Personally, I've learned a great deal about organizational structure and leadership through volunteering within the Society of Interventional Radiology (SIR). I got started by applying for a position within the newly formed Women in IR Section. As a result of my involvement, I was subsequently invited to take part in other projects, which helped to deepen my experience within and knowledge of the organization. Some of these roles included helping to construct an online mentor match platform, sitting on a newly formed Diversity & Inclusion Advisory Board, and joining the Editorial Board of our society magazine, *IR Quarterly*. Beyond the leadership experience that you'll find in medical organizations like SIR, they can also help you to meet and network with other leaders around the country. These kinds of connections will not only enrich your professional world, but they can be leveraged into other opportunities-- even a new job when you need one. It's never too soon to look for leadership opportunities.

Claim Your Role

Learning to lead can be a challenge, especially if you've ever doubted yourself before (raising my hand over here!). As you learn, claiming your role can help establish you as a leader in your own mind and the minds of your team members. As women, we walk a tightrope, balancing our ambitions with what society expects of us. But I believe we should claim the positions we've earned, by stepping off the tightrope, onto solid ground. To me, this means leading in a way that is authentically and unapologetically you. When we take ownership of our roles, our patients and communities benefit. Here's one example.

One day, I was just about jogging from one end of my department to the other-- from a nephrostomy to a lumbar puncture and back. Multiple patients were ready at the same time, and I was working as fast as I could. Outside the interventional suite, the team's lead aprons hung on a rack, with a few pegs in the middle labeled "Doc." But the rack was crowded, and the velcro of my lead stuck to others nearby, as I hurried from case to case. I coveted an unlabeled hook at the end of the rack. Off-handedly, I said to a technologist nearby, "Put 'Chief' over this hook," indicating my desired spot. She grabbed the label maker, claiming the peg for me. It might be an ostentatious little label, but I like it, and I've earned it. It not only gives me joy but helps me serve in my role. Moments like these remind me it's OK to stake my claim, take up space, and ask for what I want.

The Language of Leaders

In the challenge chapter, I talked about the languages you'll learn as a physician in training. And as a physician leader, you'll need to be multilingual. Have you ever had a conversation with an administrator or practice leader, in which you felt like they were speaking another language? The dialect of leaders speaks to teamwork and business in a way you didn't have time for when you had your nose buried in medical textbooks. But it's a powerful tool that can help you communicate about bigger, more abstract concepts than those you can access with an everyday lexicon.

This is powerful because as you walk the leadership pathway, you'll start to think about bigger challenges. As an early/mid-career leader myself, I strive to learn more of this particular language. On my commute and in my spare time, I read and listen to books and podcasts by thought leaders who focus on concepts like communication, confidence, team building, and personal development. Just as a medical career requires a commitment to life-long learning, the same is true for leadership.

Dr. Theresa Caridi, an IR with an impressive track record of leadership at the highest levels shared the following about her own evolution: "My leadership aspirations and style have changed over time. The only constant has been change, as I have continued to get to know myself well into adulthood. It is empowering to learn what I'm good at and to focus on those activities, rather than on ones that I don't particularly excel in. But it takes time and experience to figure out what those are!" As an accomplished leader at her institution and at the national level, Dr. Caridi is proof that getting to know yourself as a leader is a continuous process.

Spill Your Guts

- Do you see yourself as a leader, either now or in the future?
  - Why or why not?
- Reflect on a leadership attribute you'd like to cultivate or strengthen in yourself.
- Write down three actions you could take in order to improve, gain skills, or get mentorship in your development as a leader.

CHAPTER 9

The Inevitability of Failure

As a physician, you will be evaluated daily, not just by yourself, but by those around you. Some tests are small, like whether you pause to acknowledge the person emptying the trash. Other tests-- solving an interdepartmental conflict or passing your board exam-- carry high stakes and are inescapably public. And each time you're tested, you risk failure. It's part of the process. But because the medical field selects for high-achieving perfectionists, who've often been conditioned to believe that failure is the worst possible outcome, some of us will have a hard time accepting this fact.

I asked Arghavan Salles, MD, PhD about her own experience with failure. She shared, "I've experienced too many failures to share them all! I think one of my biggest has been being so hard on myself and those around me. In school and in training, I always expected myself to be perfect. An ugly voice in my head would taunt me if I didn't get the best possible grade, or made even a small mistake. Allowing that voice to dictate my attitude has been a huge challenge, and in my eyes, a failure. I've been working on trying to quiet this inner critic, because perfection isn't real, and striving for it is a path to sadness, not success. In a way, I wish I'd experienced failure earlier in life, so I could've come to terms with it at a younger age. Like many physicians, I didn't start experiencing it until my mid to late 20s. By then, failure seemed like a bad thing. But over time, I've realized that it's the only way we really learn. Each failure is an opportunity to grow. I just wish I'd realized that sooner."

While some struggle with perfectionism, others struggle in a system that judges us by our standardized test scores. When I asked Dr. Anna Gasparyan, a vascular surgeon in private practice about her experience with failure, she confided, "I was always a bad test-taker, so I failed the general surgery boards. They made me re-take them multiple times because I was supposed to pass them before taking the vascular boards. That failure really hung on my heart. The thing was, I never wanted to practice general surgery. I never wanted to remove another gallbladder. And at that time, the certification process was changing to reflect sub-specialization anyway. Eventually, I was able to convince them to let me take the vascular boards alone, which I passed on the first try."

She continued, "I've learned that an exam doesn't define what kind of surgeon you will be. My surgical outcomes are good, my patients love me, and I'm happy because I feel like I've found my niche. My surgeries come out so pretty, and it's really rewarding. This is what I knew I wanted to do. As a vascular surgeon, I'm living my dream." Dr. Gasparyan is an example of someone who has overcome significant obstacles to fulfill her greater purpose of serving others.

Facing Failure in Training and Beyond

In an open letter to medical students and trainees called *7 Things to Keep You Going Strong on the Path to Becoming a Doctor,* I describe some of my most cringe-worthy failures and what they've taught me. If you haven't heard it yet, you can find it by clicking on the cheerful red coffee mug on my blog, at TiredSuperheroine.com. Whether you become a procedural subspecialist or not, picking yourself up after failure is a useful skill to use throughout life. Since the medical path can be particularly challenging, the skill becomes that much more valuable.

Even after medical training, you'll experience failure as an attending too. In my experience, shame can often come along for the ride. In one of my first blog posts, I examined the many small failures I can experience on a given day. A sterile clamp drops to the floor; I waffle on the device I need next, confusing my support staff. Sometimes communication falters, or a complication occurs. And the failures aren't confined to the hospital setting-- I fail outside of work, too. I stumble over my points on a conference call, or I'm later getting home than I thought I would be. The opportunities to err are endless, even in the context of a successful career.

As I describe in my blog, these small daily gaffes can be humbling. "I whisk by the office staff, my white coat floating behind me like a polyester cape, as I stride with purpose toward my next patient. Suddenly, the hem of my coat catches a doorknob or an arm-rest and I'm yanked back, stopped in my tracks."

As I detangle myself from the office furniture, I'm embarrassed. But over time, I've learned to discard the shame that follows small slip-ups like these. It's up to you how you'll handle it "when your cape gets caught." Whether you brush off a small mistake or apologize for a larger error, it's all part of bouncing back and learning from failure. We must be kind to ourselves around our failures, given their ubiquitous nature. Avoiding excessive rumination, we can learn from each misstep, and move on. As I consider in my post, you could "whoosh your cape overhead like a superhero." Though I've never done this myself, it's symbolic of the kind of resilience I strive for as a physician, because the job demands it.

Facing Complications

When I was a fellow, one of my mentors used to remind my co-fellows and me: "If you don't have complications, you're not doing enough procedures." Meaning, complications are an inherent part of doing this kind of work; they are to be expected. It's why we carefully scrutinize the need for each procedure and name potential complications as part of the informed consent process, in which patients weigh the risks and benefits of a given procedure, according to their personal goals and values. Although complications can result from failures, I don't necessarily view them as failures themselves. But if you've ever experienced one, you know that they can certainly feel like failures regardless of the circumstances.

In training, I bore witness when a mentor of mine experienced a devastating complication. He was (and remains) one of the most meticulous people I've ever met. The case involved a kidney biopsy on a young man with compromised renal function. The biopsy was meant to determine the patient's candidacy for immunosuppressive therapy, with the hopes of reversing his disease. Without appropriate therapy, he faced worsening renal function and a future on dialysis. Several nights after the biopsy, the patient unexpectedly passed away from a delayed hemorrhage. We examined the event at our morbidity & mortality (M&M) conference to look for any potential point of improvement. Unfortunately, the patient's nephropathy placed him at an increased risk of bleeding.

No matter how well you perform, you run the risk of harming someone in your work. As you embark on a procedural or surgical pathway, this is critical to understand. Though you will strive to be as skillful and safe as you can, complications will inevitably occur. Without acceptance of this reality, you risk excessive self-flagellation, and that won't help anyone. Constructively examining the complications you encounter can be an impetus for potential improvement, but sometimes complications are unpreventable. If you find yourself struggling, it's important to seek counsel from a trusted mentor or even a grief counselor. If you try to brush complications aside, it could distract you from your next patient, or affect your mental health.

Navigating Failure at the Top of Your Field

I asked Dr. Laura Findeiss, Chief of Service for her radiology department what sort of failures she's experienced, and how she's dealt with them. "I've had lots of failures! Epic, deflating failures that really tore me down. Even now, thinking about some of them can be really hard. But I know that each of them was critical in shaping who I am and where I am in life. I truly value the lessons I took away from them. As far as navigating failure, I tend to analyze everything, and I'm my own worst critic. In the past, I've taken each experience or event apart to examine it in great detail, in order to learn which parts I have owned, and what I could have done differently."

She continued, "Failure is the best training for achieving success, if you can extract what you could have done better, or what you couldn't control but might have seen coming (to duck next time). It can even teach you how to grant yourself forgiveness. Like the calluses on your feet, the ability to forgive yourself makes it possible to walk on increasingly rough terrain over time. Success can even be dangerous if you start to think it came from you and your natural talents, rather than from the luck and other gifts that truly helped to create it. As I said to someone today, 'You need to fail to succeed.'"

She added: "Often when we often look at people who are successful, all we see is a person with influence or impact; we don't see the path they took to arrive there. Everyone has to find their own way. In general, I feel we (as successful professionals) are not usually transparent enough about the struggles that have characterized our paths. It can mistakenly lead to an impression of some sort of magic or mystery to the endpoint.

"Personally, I've had to overcome a lot. From a dysfunctional home life growing up to being a really "late bloomer," I didn't develop confidence early on. It's a double-edged sword, but if you can find the resilience that results from those challenges, you can use it to plow through the barriers you encounter, and ultimately win through determination and focus. Through my friendships with amazing, dynamic professional women, I know that many of us have had major personal struggles, and the strength we developed from those experiences actually helped create a foundation for success. In my opinion, it's important to share this reality, and to support each other in such a way that we can leverage the skills that emerge from experiences like these." Coming from a leader at the top of her field, it's encouraging and refreshing to hear how adversity and failure can actually teach us to lead more effectively if we have the right mindset.

Falling Off the Tightrope: Failing at Balance

You might worry not only about failing your patients but about failing your family as you develop a medical career. Dr. Nikki Keefe relates: "As a trainee, I brought my heart and soul to work, fully immersing myself from my surgery internship to my diagnostic and interventional radiology training. I have learned to step back slightly, as work can become all-consuming. When I've had a tough day, it's nice to be able to decompress at home, but I need to be mindful not to bring stress home to my family. There's a fine line between loving what you do and putting an undue burden on your family."

Finally, it's important to realize that as physicians, we can fail ourselves sometimes. Dr. Lara Hasan, an OB/Gyn at my hospital shared how she has experienced failure at each end of the overachiever spectrum and has needed to adjust accordingly each time. "In my past, at university, I often erred on the side of going out with friends or going away for the weekend, rather than grinding it out (with my schoolwork). Honestly, I could have had more doors open for me if I'd worked harder. I cruised through the beginning of medical school in the same way.

"But once I hit the clinical years when the hours got longer, and we were supposed to study outside of the hospital... it became a lot." Of finding the right balance, she said, "Initially, I tried to just stay in and focus on my work, but it backfired-- when I isolated myself too much, I got depressed and lonely. It was actually counterproductive. In medicine, there are so many important milestones, from clerkship exams to the USMLEs (US Medical Licensing Exams), that it's easy to think you're doing the right thing by doing nothing but studying.

"I realized I needed to maintain some kind of social connection, no matter how little time I felt like I had. So I'd meet someone to study at Starbucks or get together with friends one night per week. I realized that socializing, meeting people, and doing new things kept me sane. That's when I realized it was OK to not get the best possible grade. The extra effort needed to be at the top of the class was not worth it for me. I had to learn to balance my priorities in order to stay healthy-- mentally, physically, and emotionally."

On finding balance on the other side of training, Dr. Hasan explained, "It's easy to let this job consume you if you let it. So I strive for a personal balance, and try to create boundaries between my work and life outside of the hospital." Of the different phases of one's medical career, she remarked, "Residency is stressful because you have to get through it. And if you don't-- then what? When training was over, I felt like I'd been through a tornado. As an attending, there is a lot less pressure in some ways, and I definitely have more free time. Once you have that training under your belt, you have a variety of options to help you find your own balance. Whether it means reducing your hours, changing your job or location, there are lots of ways to achieve a balance that's right for you." Just as your career will be a dynamic journey, it's okay if achieving and maintaining a personal balance is a lifelong process.

Spill Your Guts

- What does failure mean (or look like) to you?

- Write down one or two cringe-worthy failures you've experienced, perhaps the ones you'd rather not think about. What did you learn from them?

- What does balance mean to you?

- How will you know when you've achieved it?

CHAPTER 10

Final Thoughts: You've Got This

How will it feel, and what can you accomplish when you find your place in medicine? Will you use your own two hands to fix the problems you diagnose? Will you relish the gratification of a well-sewn anastomosis or a deft intubation? Can you walk into work in high heels, and save lives? Sure!

And will you face challenges along the way as you find where you belong? I'd just about guarantee it. At some point, you'll encounter the discouraging comments of a nay-sayer. You'll sift through advice tinged with bias. Medicine is a hierarchical world, and it can be challenging to know who to listen to when it comes to choosing your career. It can be a challenge to hold onto the desires within when you're grappling with self-doubt.

As you scale the mountain that is medical training, you may occasionally look around to realize that you're the only female (or minority, or non-binary) physician around. In my field and others like it, this is a common occurrence. But when you're feeling isolated, or doubt creeps in, I hope this book can serve as a guide and provide the support you need. As a female proceduralist or surgeon, you'll stand on the shoulders of women who've come before you. They've worked to find their place in medicine, and in doing so, they've smoothed the path for you. Even across generations, we are in this together.

I hope you find how you stand out in a good way. Look inside to find and develop your unique set of strengths and talents. Your practice, your community, and our world need them. Beyond your healing hands, we need your ideas and leadership. So claim your power. Operate at the top of your license. Build a satisfying, balanced life for yourself. You'll work hard to accomplish these things, so don't forget to enjoy them.

You're a Woman Who Operates

There was a time in residency when it seemed like my attendings had all the answers. But some of them didn't understand my desire to treat emergencies and save lives. As a woman in a male-dominated sphere, I was, and sometimes still am seen as an IR in an unexpected package. Despite the challenges of being a woman in medicine, you'll soon make the transition from aspiring doctor to resident, and from trainee to attending, as the women in these pages have before you.

When I was coming of age in medicine, I didn't know what the future would hold. The one thing I knew was that I wanted to have a life outside of the hospital. I used to wonder if it was possible to have a meaningful career as a physician without sacrificing my own well-being in return. There were no female role models present to show what life in a procedural specialty might look like, or frankly, whether it was worth it to pursue a career in a male-dominated field. During those years, I had no clue whether I'd be able to build a life of service that also worked for me. I've found that not only is it possible, but this career has allowed more opportunity than I ever thought possible. And the way you build your life and practice will be wholly up to you. With the help of the different perspectives in this book, I hope you'll see how each physician can apply her own approach to achieving success and balance.

As Dr. Theresa Caridi shared: "Compartmentalizing is one of the valuable lessons I've learned along the way. When I need to work, I just work. I don't try to force my worlds to collide anymore. I can still sign my child up for a gymnastics class when I have a free moment at work. But now, I don't force anything that doesn't seem to fit. Instead of having my kids pop by the hospital to say "hi," and being pressed for time to visit, now I take those 15 minutes to knock out my dictations and get home to them. Compartmentalizing has allowed me to be more productive so that when I get home, I can be present and enjoy my kids before they go to bed. When I do this, my time at home is truly *my* time. This has been an invaluable lesson."

Since I enjoy working at our busy trauma center, my balance involves working interspersed weeks at a smaller, quieter hospital. I also reserve dedicated time to relax at home. I've found what works best for me and my family over time, and I am confident you will, too.

As you embrace your calling in medicine, I hope you find the work that lights you up. Because while modern medicine can be rife with paperwork and headaches, enjoying what you do can buoy you through the inevitable challenges. If you're as lucky as Nancy Yen Shipley, you'll find just where you belong. On finding her place in orthopaedic surgery, she recalled, "Once I figured it out, there was no turning back for me."

Finding Community

Though women have a small (but growing) foothold in the traditionally male-dominated fields, our common skills and challenges bond us across specialties. Even when we are separated geographically, we can connect more easily than ever with the help of technology. Some of my favorite colleagues practice clear across the country from me. Between our reunions at national meetings, we access each other over the phone, via email, and on social media. When you find your people in medicine, they'll be there to support you, even when you're the only woman in the room.

As Dr. Agnes Solberg, founder of the popular Radiology Chicks Facebook group attests: "The struggles of being a woman physician, especially in a male-dominated field are certainly real, but should not dissuade any woman from becoming one. Many organizations exist to help women in these fields, from my own to the American Association of Women Radiologists (AAWR), and SheMD, just to name a few. Most national medical organizations now have dedicated sections for women to come together to work on common interests, like the Women in Interventional Radiology Section of the Society of Interventional Radiology (SIR), for example. This group has made strides in increasing representation of female speakers at conferences, advocating for family leave, and promoting awareness around gender bias."

For me, becoming an empowered, fulfilled physician has often meant stepping outside of my comfort zone, continuous learning, and finding like-minded people for support. I hope this book inspires you to do the same. From my blog, TiredSuperheroine.com, to my Facebook group *Tired Superheroines*, I've gathered resources and a growing community of like-minded individuals who want to thrive in their chosen field. Sign up for my email list to hear about opportunities for group coaching and in-person retreats so we can meet and mastermind together. With our common goals and challenges, we can help each other, online and in real life. As Dr. Nancy Yen Shipley put it: "My world was enriched multi-fold once I was able to connect with other women in my specialty. Getting on social media has helped me connect with other physicians in ways I never thought possible."

As the degree of diversity in the procedural and surgical specialties improves, you'll be surrounded by increasing numbers of women who share your mission. Remember that some have already scaled the mountains you're eyeing. We can help you, pointing out the trails and the foot-holds. Sometimes, it helps just to know that someone like you has succeeded before. Other trailblazing women have helped pave the way for you, the woman who wants to operate.

Battle the Doubt and Win

If you're anything like me, you'll deal with self-doubt on your journey into medicine. Countless times I wondered whether I was good enough to train in diagnostic imaging, let alone join the enigmatic boy's club of interventional radiology.

But on the other side of training, I can assure you that it's worth battling through the doubt. You might even use it as fuel to accomplish your goals. When you do, you'll experience the privilege and gratification that comes from finding a patient's problem and fixing it with your own two hands. Practicing medicine in this way is a privilege. And if you want in, I'm personally welcoming you.

Contributors

I would like to thank the women who contributed to this book. It's a privilege to call them my friends and colleagues. The following are abridged biographies, which highlight some of their many accomplishments. To find out more and connect with them online, see their preferred social media networks, which are included below.

Theresa Caridi, MD, FSIR
is an interventional radiologist who was named a Washingtonian Top Doctor in 2018 during her time at the MedStar Georgetown University Hospital in Washington, D.C. At the time of this writing, she is transitioning to her new roles as an Associate Professor of IR, IR Division Director, and Vice-Chair of Interventional Affairs at the University of Alabama at Birmingham. On Twitter, she's @thefibroidlady.

Hannah Clode

is a third-year medical student pursuing an MD/MBA degree at the University of Miami Miller School of Medicine. She aspires to be efficient, autonomous, and joyful throughout her entire career. She likes listening too much. Her specialty choice is yet to be determined, and she plans to take a year off to consider her options, namely: IR, surgery, family medicine, and OB/GYN. On Twitter, she's @HannahClode.

Laura Findeiss, MD, FSIR, FAHA

is a Past President of the Society of Interventional Radiology. She is a Professor of Radiology and Surgery at Emory University School of Medicine and the Chief of Service for Radiology at Grady Memorial Hospital in Atlanta, Georgia. She's passionate about leading patient-centered change in healthcare and is an avid cyclist, skier, and snowboarder. On Twitter, she's @radlkf.

Anna Gasparyan, MD

is a board-certified vascular surgeon in private practice in Southern California. She specializes in endovascular & vascular surgery including the treatment of venous disease. In her free time, she enjoys quality time with her son, Bikram yoga classes, and long-distance running.

Anne "Annie" Gill, MD
is an Assistant Professor of Pediatric Interventional Radiology at the Emory University School of Medicine. She is a leader within the Women in IR Section of the Society of Interventional Radiology, in which she works to increase the gender diversity of selected speakers at national meetings. On Twitter, she's @AnneGillMD.

Lara Hasan, MD
is a board-certified obstetrician-gynecologist in private practice in Southern California. She's a world-traveler, outdoor adventurer, burgeoning cook, and trivia geek. She can be found on Instagram as @palmspringsadventurer.

Aneesa Majid, MD, MBA, FSIR
is an interventional radiologist who has spent the majority of her career in private practice. She continues to find her balance with the help of entrepreneurial endeavors since completing her MBA at the Kellogg School of Management. A leader within the Society of Interventional

Radiology (SIR), she led the development of the first Women in IR Champion Award. On Twitter, she's @nIradIR.

Natosha Monfore, DO
is an early career interventional radiologist in private practice. She is a passionate advocate for mentorship, with countless projects completed with the Residents, Fellows, & Students Section of the SIR. She continues to serve as a leader within the Women in IR Section and as a SIR delegate for the Young Physicians Section of the American Medical Association (AMA). She is on Instagram as @nmonfore.

Lola Oladini, MD, MBA
Is a rising PGY-3 IR/DR resident at Stanford Hospitals and Clinics. She aspires to be compassionate, creative, and relentless in the pursuit of leaving her community a better place than how she met it. She likes improv and baking cookies. On Twitter, she's @Dr_Lola_IR.

Arghavan Salles, MD, PhD
is an academic bariatric surgeon. A former Scholar in Residence at the Stanford Universi-

ty School of Medicine, her research focuses on gender equity, well-being, and the challenges women face in the workplace. She is an internationally recognized speaker and an activist against sexual harassment. On Twitter, she's @arghavan_salles.

Nancy Yen Shipley, MD
is an orthopaedic surgeon in private practice. She is also a mother, half of a dual-physician couple, a writer, a speaker, and a podcaster (The 6% with NancyMD). Through these roles, and her online content, she helps open doors for those that wish to BE more and DO more in their own lives. On Twitter, she's @_NancyMD.

Agnieszka Solberg, MD
is a practicing Vascular & Interventional Radiologist who is board-certified in Internal Medicine (ABIM), Nuclear Medicine (ABNM), and Radiology (ABR). She is a Clinical Assistant Professor at the University of North Dakota. A passionate advocate of women in radiology and informatics, she founded the Facebook community Radiology Chicks. On Twitter, she's @AgnesSolberg.

About the Author:

Barbara Hamilton, MD is a practicing interventional & diagnostic radiologist. She attended Rutgers, The State University of New Jersey, where she did a combined BS/MD program with the University of Medicine & Dentistry of New Jersey (UMDNJ). She completed a transitional year at Deaconess Medical Center in Spokane, Washington, then went on to a residency in diagnostic imaging at the Rhode Island Hospital of Brown University. She completed a fellowship in interventional radiology at the University of California, Los Angeles (UCLA) in Westwood, California. Hooked on the California sunshine, she found employment in Palm Springs, a small community outside of Los Angeles, where she focuses on minimally invasive therapies for trauma, malignancy, and portal hypertension.

In her early career, she has ascended into various leadership roles, including becoming Chief of Interventional Radiology and Vice-Chair of Radiology at Desert Regional Medical Center in Palm Springs. Within the Society of Interventional Radiology (SIR), she has served as Chair of the Women in IR Section, collaborating on various projects ranging from mentorship to diversity & inclusion. She is Deputy Editor of the SIR's *IR Quarterly* publication. Since becoming a mother, she's found a joyful balance between work and life outside of the hospital. She's made it her mission to promote the same for other women in male-dominated fields through her blog, TiredSuperheroine.com.

You can find her on Twitter as @TSuperheroine, on Instagram as @tiredsuperheroine, and moderating her private Facebook group, Tired Superheroines.

Resources:

Blog
To learn more about developing your career, advocating for yourself at work, and learning to lead, head to https://tiredsuperheroine.com

Facebook community
Tired Superheroines is a private group for women in male-dominated fields and their allies. It can be found at https://www.facebook.com/groups/tiredsuperheroines

In-person mastermind retreat:
Relax with and get to know other women in male-dominated and procedural subspecialties. For more information, look under the "retreat" tab at tiredsuperheroine.com. You can enter your email address to receive periodic retreat-specific updates.

The Society of Interventional Radiology's Pregnancy Toolkit can be found at:
https://www.sirweb.org/practice-resources/toolkits/pregnancy-toolkit/

About the Publishing Support Services:

Dr. Jasmine Zapata is an award winning author, radio personality, pediatrician, public health physician, mother and wife. She is also the founder of Motivational M.D. Publishing, a family-owned business that helps aspiring authors publish books that heal, uplift and inspire.

Connect with Motivational M.D. Publishing on Facebook at www.facebook.com/motivationalmdpublishing or by going to http://Imreadytolaunch.com

Special Thanks

I'd like to recognize and thank Leif Dahleen, MD, the blogger behind The Physician on FIRE (https://www.physicianonfire.com), for his sponsorship of 200 books, which will be distributed to and support young women in medicine across the nation. For your mentorship, your offer of financial education to millions of doctors, and for your support in this launch, I'm eternally grateful.

A heartfelt thanks to Guerbet, a global leader in medical imaging, pharmaceuticals, medical devices, and digital/AI solutions. As a partner helping healthcare professionals in diagnostic and interventional radiology since 1926, they are also an active advocate for gender parity in both medicine and industry. Thank you for your sponsorship in helping to launch this book in support of up and coming women in medicine.

Made in the USA
Columbia, SC
21 September 2020